CAMPFIRE GHOST STORIES

Volume II

A.S. Mott

GHOST
HOUSE
Ghost House Books

© 2004 by Ghost House Books
First printed in 2004 10 9 8 7 6 5 4 3
Printed in Canada

The Publisher: Ghost House Books
Distributed by Lone Pine Publishing

10145 – 81 Avenue
Edmonton, AB T6E 1W9
Canada

1808 – B Street NW, Suite 140
Auburn, WA 98001
USA

Website: http://www.ghostbooks.net

National Library of Canada Cataloguing in Publication

Mott, A.S. (Allan S.), 1975–
   Campfire Ghost Stories, volume II / A.S. Mott

   ISBN 13: 978-1-894877-42-8
   ISBN 10: 1-894877-42-X

   1. Ghost.   2. Tales.   I. Title.
BF1461.M68 2004   398.25   C2004-902183-4

Editorial Director: Nancy Foulds
Project Editor: Shelagh Kubish
Editorial: Dawn Loewen, Shelagh Kubish
Production Manager: Gene Longson
Cover Design: Elliot Engley
Layout & Production: Chia-Jung Chang
Illustrations: Aaron Norell

The stories, folklore and legends in this book are based on the author's collection of sources including individuals whose experiences have led them to believe they have encountered phenomena of some kind or another. They are meant to entertain, and neither the publisher nor the author claims these stories represent fact.

We acknowledge the financial support of the Government of Canada through the Book Publishing Industry Development Program (BPIDP) for our publishing activities.

PC: P5

To Joanne Bray
This time you fit.

Contents

Acknowledgments

Let it be said now, as clear and loud as the final note of a heartbreaking aria sung by a large foreign woman whose voice has been touched by the very grace of god, that this book would suck so hard were it not for the efforts of my editor, Shelagh Kubish. Not only does she possess what I am told the kids today refer to as "mad skills," she is also a fundamentally cool person to work with. She made working on this book far easier than it had any right to be.

I would also like to thank Dawn Loewen who was considerate enough to put off the birth of her first child for several days so that she could offer up her opinions on several of the stories that appear in this book. Though some have suggested to me that this was just a coincidence, I am certain that Dawn is exactly the kind of team player to make this personal sacrifice for the betterment of the book.

There are pictures in these pages and they were drawn by a genius named Aaron Norell. I have to thank him for so vividly capturing the images I had imagined while I sat typing away at my keyboard. I must also thank the *grande artistes* in the production department who transformed a medium-sized computer file into an actual honest-to-goodness book. They are Elliot Engley who created the cover and Chia-Jung Chang, whose layout made it all fit in between.

And lastly, I must thank Nancy Foulds and Shane Kennedy for their faith that I could get the job done.

Introduction

When I was younger I knew I wanted to be a writer, but it wasn't my only creative passion. I also loved the theater and easily saw myself pursuing a career as an actor or a director over one in publishing. And though I am the last person to be able to be unbiased about the level of my talent, I think it isn't unreasonable to believe that based on my marks in drama class (without which I never would have gotten into university) and the various scholarships and awards I received (which at a total of $625 amounts to my entire theatrical income to date) I might have actually been successful at it. Why then did I decide to go into the much less glamorous field of literature? Two reasons. The first was that the more I acted, the harder it was for me to fight the stage fright that hit me before every performance. During the last play I was in, I became so nervous before each show I visibly shook. The second reason can be proven by going to my author's bio on the Lone Pine Web site <http://www.lonepinepublishing.com>. There you will see photographic evidence of why if I had been an actor it would have meant a lifetime playing the hero's comic sidekick and never the actual hero himself.

By now I am certain that you are wondering why I'm telling you all this, since it doesn't seem to have much to do with campfire ghost stories, but I assure you, there is a method to my autobiographical madness. My reason for supplying you with this unnecessary information is so you understand why when I am asked to go somewhere and read aloud from one of my books, I *always* say yes. Having not acted on stage for almost a decade now, the only chance I get to relive my past dramatic glories is to read one of my stories to anyone who is willing (or forced) to listen. Because of this interest in drama I was eager to write this book, as it will give me a chance to read from a book that was meant to be read aloud.

And since I've had some experience reading ghost stories to both small and large groups of people ranging in age from 8 to 80, I thought it might be beneficial if I offered some advice to you on the best ways to perform the stories collected in this book. These simple guidelines that I follow, though, should not be taken as the definitive gospel on the art of public oration. Instead, they should be considered what they are—the personal rules that I've developed after performing both failed and successful readings.

Rule #1: Know Your Lines

While I would never suggest that you go so far as to memorize any of these stories, I do believe it would be a big mistake to read one aloud without reading it to yourself first. Even the best actors find it difficult to give a good performance while sight-reading a text, so preparation is one of the best ways to ensure an entertaining reading. Even though there are several stories I have read aloud many times, I always make sure to look over them at least once before a specific reading. If it's possible, I even go so far as to read them aloud to myself. The more you are familiar with the text, the better your performance will be, as you can spend more time focusing on how you read, rather than on what you're reading.

Rule #2: Know Your Audience

Another reason to read a story before performing it is to determine if it is the right one for the people you'll be reading it to. Having read to many different kinds of groups, I can honestly say that the biggest difference between success and failure is picking the right story for your audience. The pain that comes when you can feel the boredom growing in a room full of fourth graders is not one I want you to experience, having lived through it myself. The stories in this book have been written to satisfy a wide variety of audiences, both young and old, so choosing one at random is a risky proposition at best.

You should use not only age to determine which story you are going to read, but desired reaction as well. One of the questions I'm inevitably asked when reading for younger audiences is "What's your scariest story and can you read it to us?" While this may not seem like too difficult a request to satisfy, it always requires some judgment on my part, since different audiences are scared by different things. In my experience kids between 8 and 10 are amazingly fearless. No matter how terrifying a story you tell them, they will inevitably complain that it wasn't scary at all and then tell you in all seriousness that if they were ever confronted by a rotting flesh-eating zombie, they would just punch it in the nose. It's only around 11 or 12 that most kids become aware that they're not superheroes and that they're not as invulnerable as they once believed. This makes them much easier to scare, and much more fun to read to. Adults, on the other hand, are much more unpredictable. I've had people in their 40s complain that one of my tamest stories gave them horrible nightmares, and I've also had reactions to my nastiest stories that were as blasé as those I get from fourth graders. And sometimes you might not want to scare your audience. Not everybody likes to be frightened. That's why I've included several stories in this book that are meant to be more funny or amusing than blood chilling. Feel free to choose one of these stories if you want to entertain without frightening.

Rule #3: Read Slowly and Enunciate

This one is obvious, but it's harder to follow that most people would think. Reading in front of others is very scary. Statistically it is the most common fear people share, more than snakes, heights, closed-in spaces or even death itself. As I mentioned earlier, I, myself—who *liked* to act in front of others—used to become so afraid before a performance I would become nauseous and shake uncontrollably. Because many people have this fear of public reading, they often make the mistake of trying to get it over with as soon as possible. While this approach might make it easier for them to get through, it doesn't do anything for the audience. The best way to overcome your anxiety is to deliver a good performance and earn the adulation that comes from it, so make sure you speak as slowly and clearly as your nerves allow. But also remember to not read *too* slowly or you might put your audience to sleep.

Rule #4: Dialogue Is Your Friend

If you are reading a story loaded with dialogue, do not make the mistake of reading it all in the same way. If, for example, a story tells you that a particular character has a deep booming voice, then—by all means—give his or her dialogue as much bass as you can muster. You don't have to become Rich Little, but the more work you put into making the characters different, the more the audience is likely to get out of the experience. This is a good reason to follow rule #1. If you've read the story before, you'll have a better idea how the characters should sound.

Rule #5: Avoid Carbonated Beverages

Reading aloud can make a person quite thirsty, so having a glass of water on hand is recommended. However, it isn't a good idea to drink soda pop while you're reading to others. Even though a good loud belch *will* get you an animated reaction from your audience, it's not quite the one you want to aim for. Seriously. I'm talking from experience here.

Rule #6: Aim for the Cheap Seats

Since campfire ghost stories are not renowned for their exquisite subtlety, do not feel as though you should give a dignified and low-key performance. Ham it up. Go for the gusto. If a story requires you to make a weird noise, then go all out in making it. If a story requires you to scream, then rattle the windows. This isn't art; it's fun, so be as animated as you can be. Chances are if you feel like an idiot, you're doing something right.

Truthfully, though, people spend whole lifetimes learning how to do this sort of thing properly, so feel free to do whatever works for you. If you find that doing everything the opposite of how I've just suggested gets you the reaction you're aiming for, then keep it up. However you do it, I'd love to hear from you and find out how your readings went. Let me know by e-mailing me at <asmghost-writer@yahoo.ca>. I look forward to hearing from you and finding out which stories people enjoy the most.

—A.S. Mott

You Are Here

Anson was lost. It was dark out, but luckily the moon shone brightly enough above his head for him to make out what the large map on the bulletin board on the side of the trail said. A big red star told him where he was. YOU ARE HERE it explained to him. Anson looked up to check out his surroundings and to see how they fit within the context of the map.

"I have to go north," he whispered to himself, trailing his finger along the identified route. Feeling better, he turned around and started walking in what he prayed was the right direction. He cursed himself for not bringing a flashlight. The trees that lined the trail obscured the moonlight, and the resulting darkness was unnerving. It didn't help that beyond the trees he heard the sounds of animals moving and communicating with each other. He wished they would be quiet, as each rustled leaf made him tense up for fear of what might leap out at him. He was not used to the wilderness and his only defense in the case of—say—a sudden bear attack would be to fall on the ground in a terrified heap, cover his head with his hands and cry. Unable to see more than a few inches ahead of him, he hesitated with every step, which made him feel as though he was walking backwards rather than forwards. No matter how much he squinted at it, he couldn't make out the time on his watch, so each passing minute felt like an agonizing eternity.

Every now and then he would shout out a cry for help as well as the names of his friends, who were probably snuggled warmly in their sleeping bags, oblivious to his absence. He had no idea what had possessed him to take a hike out on the trail by himself. It was light out when he had left their campsite, but after an hour it was nearly pitch-black—save for the moonlight. He became hopelessly lost, and if not for the map he had just found, he would still have no idea where he was.

He couldn't believe how much the darkness and his own unease could slow the passage of time. It felt as if he had been walking for hours and hours, but the absence of dawn and the short distance he had walked proved that that couldn't be true. He was glad that it was warm out. He couldn't imagine how horrible this situation would be if it were raining or cold or both. He shouted out several more times, but—once again—no one responded. He was beginning to think he was going insane when he spotted someone holding a flashlight in the distance.

"Hey!" he shouted, trying to capture the person's attention. Whoever it was didn't respond. "Hey! Can you hear me?" he shouted again. Still getting no response, he started to run toward the figure. As he was out of shape, his lungs began to burn as he raced to catch up. Slowly he got closer and closer to the figure, until finally he was right behind it.

"Excuse me." He tapped the stranger on the shoulder. The stranger turned and Anson screamed when he saw the man's face. It looked as it some large animal had made a feast out of it. The man's skin was torn and chunks of flesh dangled and swung with his every movement. The man's eyes were gone, his sockets empty black holes that stared out sightlessly at Anson, who turned and ran away from the mutilated stranger. He ran until his legs and lungs couldn't work anymore. He collapsed to the ground and fought a long battle to reclaim his breath. His body was so exhausted it demanded that he close his eyes, and as soon as he did he fell into a deep sleep.

🕷 🕷 🕷

It was still dark when he woke up. His legs ached, and his chest throbbed with pain, but he managed to lift himself up. He found himself back at square one. He had no idea where he was. He walked slowly and cautiously for several minutes before he came upon a map on a bulletin board along the trail. He looked at it and realized it was the same one from earlier. YOU ARE HERE it told him, the red star in the exact same place it had been before.

"North," he mumbled to himself. "Gotta go north."

He turned north and started to walk before he remembered the image of the stranger's face. He stopped, unsure if he should continue. There was no way a living person could look like that. This path was haunted, and if he started going in the same direction he had before then there was a good chance he'd meet up with the mutilated stranger once again. But the only other option would be to go the other way and that would lead him nowhere. Weighted down by his indecision, he stood in one spot for a long time before he was able to decide what to do next. Finally, he started walking north.

Even though the stranger might still be out there, Anson had realized that the ghost-zombie-whatever-the-guy-was had made no move to attack him and it was only the shock of the man's appearance that had caused him to run away in the first place. Wanting to get back to his friends, he figured that if he did run into the stranger again, he would just ignore him.

Before he entered the part of the trail that was covered by trees and allowed for little moonlight, he checked out his watch to see what time it was. He was shocked to see that it had been only two hours since he had left his friends. He shook his watch and raised it to his ear. It had stopped ticking. It was broken, so gave him no clue whether it was minutes or hours until dawn.

Disheartened, he started walking again. Just as it had before, time slowed to a standstill and the minutes passed like hours. He tried to walk as fast as he could, but he never sensed that he was making any real progress. Up ahead he saw someone with a flashlight. Fearing that it might be the stranger, he made no attempt to approach, but as he walked he saw that the light was moving toward him. The person with the flashlight was walking in his direction and it would be a matter of minutes before he passed by him.

Anson's stride became unsteady as he moved closer to the figure. He didn't want to be afraid, but he was. His heart beat faster and faster with each footstep. It was all he could do not to turn around and start running.

"There's nothing to be scared of," he insisted to himself, but he didn't believe it.

But then—as the figure grew closer and closer—he could see that the person with the flashlight was not the supernatural figure he had encountered before. It was a young woman, who looked just as scared as he was.

"Excuse me," she shouted when she saw him, "but I'm lost and need some help!"

"Me too," he answered her.

They walked directly toward each other and the woman shined her flashlight into his face to check him out. To Anson's shocked amazement she began to scream.

"W-w-what are you?" she cried out with fear.

Before he could answer, she turned and started to run. As she ran away from him, he saw that the back of her jacket was torn and soaked with blood.

"Wait," he shouted out to her, "you're hurt! Let me help!"

She didn't stop. She kept on running.

"What was that about?" he wondered to himself.

Not having an answer, he kept walking. It felt like forever, but eventually he came across another bulletin board with a map on it. Excited to finally have another clue about his location he ran to it and checked it out. What he found made no sense. There once again was a red star telling him YOU ARE HERE, but it was in the exact same place it had been on the other bulletin board. He felt that he was going crazy. He was certain he hadn't gone in a circle, but as he looked up and checked out his surroundings he was shocked to see that he was in the same spot as before.

Tears of frustration rolled down his face as he slumped down to the ground and started to weep. What was happening? Why would this night not end?

As soon as Anson's friends noticed that he hadn't come back from his hike, they started searching for him. By the time dawn arose, they still hadn't found him. They went and found the camp ranger and within a couple of hours an official search party was organized to find him. The search lasted for days, until he was finally found.

It was the ranger who had to explain to his friends what had happened to Anson.

"Sometime during his hike, an animal attacked him. Based on the wounds, I'd have to say it was a bear. From what I saw I'm pretty sure he died instantly, so he didn't suffer. It appears that his watch was broken during the attack, so we have a good idea when it happened, which was just two hours after he left your campsite." He paused and let Anson's friends absorb this horrible news, but when the silence became too powerful he started talking again. "This may surprise you but this is only the third animal attack that's occurred in this forest since I started working here 14 years ago. The first one was an older man, who had gotten his face savaged real badly, and the other was a younger woman who had gotten attacked from behind..." he started to say more before he realized he wasn't helping by being so descriptive.

Anson refused to move from his spot by the bulletin board. It felt as if he had been sitting there for days, but still the sun hadn't risen and the night inexplicably continued.

"Dawn has to come," he kept telling himself over and over again. "Dawn has to come and my friends will find me. If I stay here long enough, they will find me."

The Contract

Geoff sat nervously in the waiting room to his boss' office. Even though the room was kept warm, his anxiety made him shiver. Normally such a situation would have him sweating like a chicken on a rotisserie, but for some reason his skin felt only the slightest bit damp. It felt as if he had been sitting there forever. He had trouble even remembering what he had been doing before he had been summoned.

"Do you know what this is about?" he asked Lola, Mr. Friedmont's secretary, but, just like the previous four times he asked her this question, she appeared not to hear him.

Her telephone rang and she picked it up.

"Yes, sir," Geoff heard her say into the receiver. She then turned toward him and spoke to him for the first time since he had sat down. "You can go in now," she told him, her words tinged with an inexplicably icy disdain that made him worry even more about what he must have done wrong.

Mr. Friedmont was on the phone when Geoff walked into his office.

"Don't give me some sob story about your mother's medical bills," the large man shouted at the other person on the line. "If you don't pay me back what you owe me by the end of the week, then I'm taking your car, your house and that pathetic excuse of a restaurant you have the nerve to call a business!" With that he slammed down his phone. "Damn relatives," he swore under his breath before he noticed the cowering employee standing in front of him.

"Sit down, Dixon," he ordered Geoff, using his last name, "I was just finishing up some business with my sister."

Geoff sat down in the small, uncomfortable chair in front of Mr. Friedmont's desk. It was so low to the ground that he had to look up to see his boss' face. There, among a yellowing mustache, a newly sprouted pimple and a large, unambiguous nose, he found the one thing no one ever wanted to see on George Friedmont's fleshy visage— a big toothy grin. Everyone knew that, like a shark, Mr. Friedmont smiled only when he smelled blood in the water and was about to go in for the kill.

"Do you know why I called you in here?" he asked Geoff, his disturbingly cheerful smile still apparent on his face.

"No, sir," Geoff admitted.

Hearing this, Mr. Friedmont interlaced his fingers and sat back in his seat, striking the pose of an armchair philosopher.

"I am certain that you are aware that I am a very rich man," he said.

"Yes, sir," Geoff nodded.

"Do you know how I was able to earn all my wealth?"

"No, sir," Geoff shook his head.

"I was able to do it because I believe in following the rules. When I sign a contract with someone I make sure I follow every clause that contract contains, and I make sure that the other person does the same." With that Mr. Friedmont unclasped his hands and leaned forward in his chair, readying himself for the kill. "Have you ever read the contract you signed when you became an employee at this company?" he asked Geoff, even though he knew the answer.

"No, sir," Geoff admitted. The truth was that the day he was hired, the director of personnel had him sign so many documents he wasn't even sure which contract Mr. Friedmont was referring to.

"Then I suppose you think that that absolves you, don't you?" asked Mr. Friedmont.

Geoff gulped.

"Absolves me of what, sir?"

"Of breaking the rules and trying to get out of our agreement!!" Mr. Friedmont roared at him, his face turning into a burning hot scarlet mask of anger.

"I don't know what you're talking about," Geoff said, trying to defend himself.

"Oh you don't, do you? You don't know what I'm talking about?" Mr. Friedmont reached into his desk and pulled out a file folder. "This is what I'm talking about!" he shouted as he threw the folder at Geoff. Papers and photographs spilled out of the folder and fell to the floor as Geoff fumbled to catch it. "Take just one look and you'll understand why you're in breach of contract."

Geoff picked up the papers and photographs that were on the ground and tried to tidy them up before he looked at them. Mr. Friedmont grew impatient at this and roared at him to get on with it. Geoff looked down at the first page in front of him. It looked like a police report. What it said left him confused. A final paragraph at the bottom of the page summed up the report's findings:

Mr. Dixon's body was found hanging from an electrical cord in his basement. All the available evidence, including the note he left behind, lead us to conclude that his death was a suicide.

"What does this have to do with me?" Geoff asked uneasily.

"Look at one of the damn photos, you moron," his boss swore at him.

Geoff found one of the photographs and gasped aloud when he saw it. There in the picture, as clear as day, was his body hanging from an electrical cord from a beam in his small basement. Now more confused than ever, he shuffled through the papers until he found a photocopy of a handwritten note. Looking at it he could see the original had been written on the personalized stationery his sister had given him last Christmas. The note read:

I can't take the pressure anymore. I'm so lonely and this job is killing me, so I've decided this is my only way out. I'm sorry. Please forgive me.

—Geoff

"Did you really think you could get out of your contract so easily?" sneered Mr. Friedmont.

"I don't understand," Geoff answered, fear and panic evident in his words.

"Your contract specifically states that the only way you are legally able to leave this company is by serving out the agreed-upon term of 10 years or by being fired." Mr. Friedmont reached back into his desk and pulled out another folder. This one contained the contract that Geoff had signed when he started at the company. "*Nowhere* in this document," he explained to Geoff, "does it say that death is a legitimate way to terminate your contract. *NOWHERE!* You have another eight years to work at this company, regardless of whether or not you're dead!"

"What are you talking about?" Geoff stood up and shouted at his boss.

"Just look at yourself, you fool," Mr. Friedmont pulled a small mirror out of his desk and handed it to the quivering mass of nerves in front of him.

Geoff grabbed the mirror, looked into it and nearly fainted. No doubt about it, he was looking at a dead man. "H-h-h—" he stammered as he stared at his reflection.

"How? It's all in your contract, that's how. It says clearly that if you die before the contract has been fulfilled, then I have every right to uses the powers of Darknyss and Evyl, my lawyers, to resurrect you and keep you alive as an animated corpse until the end of the agreed-upon term. Normally this would mean you'd have to work here another eight years, but thanks to the Suicide Penalty Clause, I have the right to add another 100 years to time left in the contract."

"One hundred years! But you won't even be alive by then!"

"You're assuming I'm alive right now," answered Mr. Friedmont. "You're not the only one who has signed a contract you know. I have 300 years to go before I'm eligible to pass on."

"But—" Geoff attempted to speak before Mr. Friedmont interrupted him.

"How do I manage to look so good for someone so dead? You'd be amazed by what someone trained in the arts of plastic surgery, taxidermy and undertaking can do for the deceased. I look better now than when I was alive. Which can't be said for some of the other dead folks working here. You can't tell me you didn't notice them."

Geoff had seen some people in the building who hadn't looked particularly healthy, but he had never once thought that they were the walking dead. "But, but..." he tried to speak again, but he was unable to think of anything to say.

"Don't act all surprised!" Mr. Friedmont scolded him. "You knew what you were getting into. I mean, you signed the contract with your own blood, after all."

"No, I didn't!" Geoff protested. He would have remembered doing something as suspicious as that.

"Sure you did. Remember how we made you take that insurance physical? Well, during that we took some of your blood and placed it inside the ink cartridge that was in the pen you used to sign everything with. It's standard procedure at this company. It's not my fault if you people don't look out for yourselves."

Geoff slumped down dejectedly into the chair in front of Mr. Friedmont's desk.

"You said it was possible for me to get fired?" he asked hopefully.

"Yes, but in this case it means we'd throw you into the boiler room furnace." Mr. Friedmont stood up and walked over to Geoff. He grabbed his arm and lifted the stunned zombie out his chair and led him to his office door.

"I suggest you just do your best to do a good job and the 108 years will fly by like nothing. Now get back to work and tell Henson that if his work rate doesn't improve soon then he's looking at a fast trip to the boiler room." With that he pushed Geoff out of his office and slammed his door shut.

Geoff stood for a while as he tried to figure out what had just happened. Finally, Lola noticed his confusion and made the uncharacteristic attempt to cheer him up.

"Don't worry about it," she said to him. "Being dead isn't as bad as people make it out to be. I've been dead for five years now and I've never felt better! You will have to get used to the constant craving for live human brains, but they have a patch for that now and, in a pinch, you can always buy fresh cow brains at the butcher shop around the corner."

"Thanks," Geoff mumbled as he started to shuffle out of the waiting room and back to his cubicle. As he slowly stumbled on his dead legs past his coworkers, he noticed that he honestly couldn't tell the difference between the ones who were dead and who were still alive.

This didn't make him feel any better.

A Barrel of Monkeys

One can hardly imagine the stench that emanated from the large wooden barrel that Alonzo Degas kept hidden in the forest behind his backyard. It was a nauseatingly strong one-two punch of rot and decay that hit the nose with such a wallop it could easily knock a person out. If it is possible for a smell to be judged on a moral scale, then this one was pure evil, without any redeeming social value whatsoever.

Alonzo was an animal trainer who specialized in working with monkeys. For eight months of the year he would travel throughout North America and perform his act at state and county fairs and even at the occasional birthday party. Amused by his monkeys' acrobatic antics, Alonzo's audiences always laughed and applauded at the end of his shows, but they would have been less appreciative if they had known exactly how Alonzo trained his primate performers.

Armed with a powerful cattle prod, he would make the monkeys rehearse their routines over and over again, punishing their every mistake with a painful shock to the ribs. If he had tried this with a monkey straight out of the wild, then this sort of treatment would have likely got him killed, but he avoided such danger by buying older monkeys who had been bred in captivity for scientific research. Their teeth were pulled out, their claws were removed, and they were kept so weak from hunger they were too listless to fight back. With this combination of brutality and neglect, it was only natural that

Alonzo frequently had to deal with the death of one of his animals. If a monkey died while he was on tour, he would usually just throw the poor creature into a cardboard box, place the box in a garbage bag and toss it into a nearby dumpster. This disposal method was illegal, of course, but he had yet to be caught.

If a monkey died while he was at home, then its remains were taken to the barrel in the woods. It's no wonder, then, that the thing smelled so bad, as it contained eight rotting monkey corpses.

Alonzo never felt guilty about how he treated his animals. To him they were simply a way to make a good living, and he never developed any kind of emotional attachment to them. He didn't even bother to give them names. He just made them wear collars with numbers on them, and referred to each one by its number. If, for example, number seven died, then the replacement monkey he bought would get the collar and become the new number seven.

If anybody had ever suggested to Alonzo that he was a monster for the way he treated his animals, he would have scoffed. His excuse for treating them so badly was that they had all been bred for medical research, which meant they likely would have spent their lives suffering anyway. At least with him they got to know the affection of the audience and weren't deliberately given cancer or anything. This argument probably wouldn't wash with most people, but it was enough to keep Alonzo's conscience clear.

After a three-month tour through June, July and August, Alonzo brought his monkeys back home to retrain them before he took them out on the road again.

He was two short, as numbers three and six had died during the tour. He bought two new ones from his regular source and started the long process of training them. It took a lot of hard work to get them to learn the routine. At home he spent easily 12 hours a day at it—6 on the road—working for months until the new arrivals were show ready. A wiser man might have considered all this effort a reason to go easy on the animals, for the longer they lived the less time he would have to spend training replacements, but the punishment method was the only one Alonzo bothered to try.

To his chagrin, the two new arrivals were so old, he wondered if they would even live long enough to become show ready. His doubts proved justified when the new number six died two weeks later. With a heavy sigh, he took the dead animal to the barrel in the forest. As he carried it, he noticed for the first time the strange gray patch of fur on its back. To his eyes it almost looked like some sort of symbol, one he had never seen before. But, once he dumped the corpse into the barrel, he forgot all about it and went back to his house, where he called his supplier and berated him for selling him such a pathetic animal.

As it turned out, Alonzo had been right. The patch of gray fur on the monkey's back was indeed a symbol, but if he had known what the symbol meant, chances are he would have started running. The gray symbol was the sign of Jhwinbatwa, an ancient African god who had served as protector of the monkeys long ago. Even before the pyramids were built, many tribes worshipped Jhwinbatwa and honored him with the finest sacrifices, but as the centuries passed, he was forgotten and his power faded away to almost nothing. Now, constantly tired and struggling to exist, he lived as a hermit in a jungle no man had ever safely walked through alone. No longer able to protect his beloved monkeys as he once had, he had decided to bless one monkey with his mark every decade. That monkey had the right to ask him for anything it desired.

Jhwinbatwa was sleeping when the dead number six visited him in his dreams.

"Greetings, old one," the monkey saluted him.

"Greetings to you," Jhwinbatwa answered.

"I am afraid to admit that I never used to believe in you," said the monkey. "My mother used to tell me that I was blessed with your mark, but I thought she was just making fun of me. If I had known the truth, I would have called on you sooner. As it is, I cannot ask you to protect me, as I am already dead, but I would be honored if you would do me the favor of avenging my death."

Jhwinbatwa listened to the monkey and asked for the details of his death. The monkey then told him about Alonzo and how his cruelty had caused so many of his kindred to suffer. Jhwinbatwa was horrified by what he heard. He grew enraged as the monkey explained in detail all of Alonzo's crimes. Before the monkey could finish, the old god screamed out with anger.

"How could I have gone so long without knowing this monster existed?" he shouted at himself. "Have I grown so feeble I must allow one of my protected to die before I could learn of this horror?" He shook his head with sadness. "I am sorry, my friend, that I could not help you sooner, but I swear by the symbol on your back that your death will not have been in vain. We both shall make certain this monster will not kill again."

"How is it to be done?" asked the monkey.

Jhwinbatwa told him.

Lying at the top of the now-filled barrel, the corpse of the blessed monkey jolted back to life as consciousness reentered the old and broken body. He felt stronger now than he ever had before. He felt claws grow back on his fingers and teeth emerge from his gums. He stood up and looked down at the pile of dead comrades on which he had rested.

"Wake up and arise," he commanded them. "This should never have been your fate! Wake up and let us take our revenge on the monster that enslaved us, starved us and tortured us with great bolts of lightning from his magic stick! Wake up and be stronger than you ever were! Wake up and save our still-suffering kin!"

Slowly, as the daylight faded and the full moon rose high into the night sky, the other monkeys awoke from their deathly slumber and rose out of the barrel. Jhwinbatwa's magic was not strong enough to restore their bodies to what they had been in life, but he gave them strength as well as claws and teeth. Knowing that they had been blessed with the chance to get even for the pain that had been inflicted on them, they began to whoop and holler into the night. They jumped and clapped and salivated at the thought of how good their torturer's flesh was going to taste in their mouths.

Alonzo, finished training for the day, had just put the last of his monkeys to bed in the small cages he kept them

in when they weren't working. Tired and ready to eat and watch some television, he threw a frozen dinner into the microwave for five minutes and then sat down to eat in front of a football game. Before he could take a bite, he heard the sound of monkeys shrieking in the distance. Reflexively he jumped out of his easy chair and ran to the room where his animals were caged. He was relieved to find that all of them were still there, but he was confused and wondered what else could have made that very distinctive sound. He ran back to the TV and flipped around the channels to see if he could find a news story about a group of animals escaping from a zoo or circus, but all he found was the usual daily programming.

He wondered if maybe the noise was being made by some forest animals that sounded like monkeys, but when he racked his brain for some idea about what kind of animal that could be, he came up blank. Something about the shrieks got under his skin and made his body tingle with nervous apprehension. The sound was getting louder with each passing second, as if growing closer to him. He ran to his door and locked it. He then turned around and ran to the bathroom, grabbing the shotgun he kept on the top shelf of the hall closet on his way. He loaded it and threw as many spare bullets as he could into his pockets. The shrieks grew louder still and now sounded as if they were coming from just outside his house.

He held his gun close to him as he waited for something for happen. The seconds passed like hours, and suddenly there was silence. The shrieking stopped. Instead of making him feel safer, the silence only terrified him more. He knew what the silence meant. It was time for the serious business to begin.

A window exploded to his right. He turned and shot at it. The blast hit something that fell to the floor with a hard thud. He cautiously walked over to it and saw that it was the monkey he had thrown into the barrel earlier that day.

"I could have sworn you were dead," Alonzo whispered to the small corpse, which was shot through with a large bullet wound. "I guess you are now."

Just then he heard the sound of a window breaking in another room. He turned and aimed his gun toward the hallway and lost sight of the dead monkey on the floor. If he had kept looking at it, he would have been shocked to see the bullet wound he had inflicted shrink and fade away. The monkey's eyes opened, and it began to shriek.

Alonzo turned back toward it and nearly fainted. Another window crashed open somewhere in the house. Then another and another. His front door burst open and revealed the living skeleton that was the first monkey to be dumped into the barrel. Alonzo began to scream and tried to shoot it, but the zombie animal jumped out of the way.

Too terrified to think, Alonzo started to shoot at everything that moved, but the dead monkeys were too fast for him to aim at, and even if he did hit them, it did no good. Within seconds he was surrounded by all nine of them. Together they shrieked and clapped and jumped. He could see that one of them had gotten ahold of the cattle prod he had used to train them. He collapsed to the floor with pain when the smiling creature jabbed it into his ribs, sending a quick jolt of electricity into his gut. His torment made them jump and clap and shriek even louder. They each took turns zapping him with the prod until he fell limp and silent on the floor. It was then that they bared their newfound teeth and claws and jumped on top of him. Though barely conscious, he felt the excruciating pain as they sunk their fangs into him and tore off chunks of his flesh with their sharp claws.

They did not stop until all that was left was a sickening collection of flailed meat and scattered bones. Finished with Alonzo, they ran and freed their living brothers, who shrieked and clapped and jumped with joy. All together they ran back to the dark forest, the moon still full in the sky. The living monkeys thanked their fallen kin for coming back to save them, and the dead monkeys reminded them to thank Jhwinbatwa. They did so, and as a reward were given back their teeth and their claws, which they would need to survive in the forest.

Their job done, the dead monkeys walked back to the barrel and climbed in, as they knew no other resting place. The blessed monkey got in last and felt a pride he had never known before as he closed his eyes. His consciousness floated away, out of his body and ever upward as if it were a balloon caught in a gentle breeze. This, he knew, was how a monkey should really feel.

By the Power of Three

Zoë was so angry she couldn't speak. She tried, but her words just sputtered uselessly out of her mouth in a nonsensical torrent. Her boyfriend, Toby, just stared down at his feet as she screamed at him. He was used to feeling the full brunt of her powerful temper. Today she was screaming at him because he had gone to get some cigarettes at the local corner store and had failed to ask her if she had wanted anything.

"Just once I would like you to show me some consideration!" was one of the few sentences she shouted at him that he was able to understand.

Even though Toby loved Zoë and had grown used to her irrational tirades, he decided then and there that he had had enough. While she screamed at him, he picked up an empty vase from the small table he was standing next to and threw it as hard as he could against the wall to his right. His actions startled Zoë and left her speechless.

"I'm sorry I had to do that," Toby said. "I promise you I'll buy you a new vase just like that one, but I had to do something to get you to quiet down, because I have something I want to say to you."

Still startled, Zoë nodded and let Toby continue.

"Zoë," Toby shook his head sadly, "I love you, but I can't take any more of your crazy outbursts. You're giving me ulcers. It has gotten to the point where every time I take a breath I'm afraid I might have done something to set you off."

"What are you saying?" she asked, not wanting to hear what she knew was his answer.

"I'm leaving you."

Zoë started screaming at him. Toby just turned around and walked out of the house. He didn't come back for his things until a few days later when he knew she wasn't going to be there. Once he had collected everything that she hadn't destroyed while he was gone, he left behind his keys and a note telling her where he could be reached in case anyone was looking for him.

Zoë was—predictably—furious. She tore up every picture she could find of Toby and burned every little memento she had that reminded her of him. It did little good. As much as she tried to hate him, she still loved him and wanted him to come back. She let a month pass before she called him, and although he was polite to her he made it very clear that he wouldn't meet with her to talk. He explained to her that he had met someone else and that he was very much in love.

Zoë was devastated. She could not believe he had found someone to replace her so quickly. She had asked him who this new woman was, but he refused to tell her, as he was afraid that Zoë might try to do something to **hurt** her.

Needing to know who had replaced her in her beloved's heart, Zoë decided to stake out the address Toby had left with her. Hiding behind a large bush she stood for hours waiting for him and his new girlfriend. Unfortunately when they finally showed up, a branch obscured the woman's face and Zoë was afraid that moving it might bring attention to herself. All she could see was that the woman had curly, strawberry blonde hair that hung down to her waist and that she dressed like a new millennium flower child.

Annoyed that she had waited for so long for so little, Zoë went home and fumed. In her mind she pictured what the woman looked like and she hated her. She was far too pretty and her hair was just too gorgeous to even consider. Great green gobs of jealousy began to flow through her veins as she happily imagined horrible things happening to her mysterious rival.

Unable to sleep, she turned on her TV and started to watch an old film on one of those channels that seemed to only play bad B movies no one remembered. This one was about a man who used the ancient powers of voodoo to get rid of his enemies and move up in the world of big business. Watching the movie Zoë remembered a small shop in the mini-mall that she always passed by on her way to work. It was called A Wicca Good Time, and as far as she could tell, it specialized in books and materials devoted to the magic arts of witchcraft. Thinking of ways to rid herself of her competition for Toby's affections, she wondered if maybe this strange little store might be the place to find a solution.

The next afternoon, during her lunch break, she walked into the little store, which appeared to be empty. It looked exactly as she had imagined. Books were everywhere, beside jars that were filled with different powders and dried animal parts. There was a section devoted to crystals and another full of various trinkets and charms. A young woman appeared from behind a curtain in the back. Zoë was too busy looking around to notice what she looked like.

"Can I help you?" asked the woman.

Zoë turned and saw that the woman was a pretty blonde with long hair tied up into an elaborate braid. Her face was friendly and conveyed a natural kindness.

"I want to hurt someone," Zoë admitted bluntly.

"You're joking, right?" asked the woman.

"No, I'm serious. I figured you witchy types could give me some kind of spell that would do something horrible to the tramp who stole my boyfriend."

"You'll find nothing like that here," the woman told her. "Don't you know about the Power of Three?"

"The Power of the what?"

"The Power of Three. It is the rule by which all Wiccas live. For every negative act we create through our magic, we will personally feel its effects threefold."

"Huh?"

"If I made a spell that turned you blind, then I would not only lose my sight, but two other senses as well. It's karma's way of keeping us positive."

"You realize you guys are nuts, right?"

"Get out of my store," ordered the woman.

"Fine," Zoë rolled her eyes. "It's not like you were going to be able to help me anyway. Fruitcake," she muttered disdainfully under her breath.

Despite her insults, Zoë still believed that casting a spell would be the best way for her to get the revenge she desired. But, having alienated the only local purveyor of books and supplies she needed, she was forced to search for what she wanted on the Internet. From her home computer she ordered six books, which arrived on her doorstep three weeks later. She pored over them as quickly as she could, but it took her eight hours before she found the kind of spell she had been looking for.

To cast the spell, she needed to do some more shopping on the Internet. When the ingredients finally arrived, they were not the finest smelling products you could buy. In fact they smelled so awful, she was amazed the mail carrier actually got them to her door. Trying not to inhale through her nose, she opened the package and removed several small jars. Inside the different jars were the dried remains of a large bullfrog, powdered monkshood, mud from the bottom of a Louisiana swamp and a severed frostbitten toe from Canada. She was most worried that if the ingredients smelled so bad now, they would smell horrible when she boiled them all together, as the spell demanded.

Her fears were justified. It was all she could do to not vomit or pass out as she stirred the concoction and read the corresponding incantation aloud. The language was tricky, but she had rehearsed it several times over a week to make sure she got it right.

Originally she had planned to find a spell that would just get rid of her unknown rival outright, but she quickly found out that in magic you had to do things in roundabout ways. You couldn't just perform a spell that killed a person; you had to do one that led to a situation in which death would be a likely result. So the spell she chose was one that made her target incredibly accident-prone. The poor woman wouldn't be able to walk two steps without potentially falling down an open manhole or getting hit by a plummeting piece of space debris or being the victim of any of a million other fatal disasters.

Zoë was amused by the randomness of the spell. It was fun for her to imagine just what the accident might end up being.

After she finished the spell, she quickly disposed of the brew she had concocted, but even a week later the smell refused to go away, no matter what she threw at it. Still, it was a small price to pay. She started calling Toby to ask him how he was doing. For several weeks he was as happy as he could be, still very much in love with his new girlfriend. Zoë was growing impatient and was beginning to feel foolish for buying into all that hocus-pocus nonsense, but then one weekend afternoon she called Toby and got no answer. She called him later that evening and he still wasn't there. For three days she couldn't get ahold of him, and she grew more excited with each passing hour, as the reason for his absence became clearer and clearer to her.

Finally, four days later, he answered his phone.

"Hello?" he sounded dead tired and extremely depressed.

"Hi Toby," she chirped cheerfully, "how are you doing?"

On the other end she heard him sigh and start to cry.

"What's the matter?" Zoë asked him, the concern in her voice masking the smile on her lips.

"It's Shanra," he explained, "she had an accident and has been in a coma for the past four days."

"Oh my goodness, that's horrible," Zoë said sympathetically as she silently began to bounce up and down with happiness. "What do the doctors say?"

"They say it's touch and go. She could snap out of it at anytime, but the longer she stays comatose the likelier it will be that she won't wake up."

"What happened?"

"You would never believe me," he answered truthfully.

"Try me."

"We were shopping for groceries and she wanted to get some peanut butter, so she walked up to a display at the end of the aisle where all the jars were stacked and picked one up. She had to step on her tiptoes to get it and the floor was wet because someone had dropped a bottle of juice and it hadn't been cleaned it up yet, and she slipped. She fell face first into the display and caused all the jars of peanut butter to crash down onto her head. It all happened so quickly; I couldn't do anything to stop it. One second she was reaching up and the next she was limp and unconscious on the floor."

Zoë gasped with mock horror and spent the next hour reassuring Toby that everything was going to turn out okay. When she finally let him go, she ran to her stereo and played the song she had always considered to be theirs (even though she had never actually mentioned it to him). She sang along with it, knowing that very soon he would be returning to her.

She was still singing the song when she drove to work the next day. In fact, she got so into it, she didn't notice the large semi that swerved in front of her. Distracted, she rear-ended it when it came to a sudden stop in front of her to avoid hitting a jaywalker. Her airbag burst open and kept her conscious long enough to see the sky rain peanut butter down upon her.

Toby was stunned when he walked into his girlfriend's hospital room and saw that Zoë lay in the other bed. "What happened?" he asked a nurse.

"You'd never believe me," she shook her head.

"Try me."

"Poor woman crashed into the back of a Jollyfun Peanut Butter truck. The accident itself wasn't too bad, but the impact caused the truck's doors to burst open and her car was hit by hundreds of jars of crunchy peanut butter."

Toby turned white.

"I've got to sit down," he said before he fainted.

Zoë felt good. She knew she was dreaming, but it was a good dream. She was in a beautiful meadow and birds were singing and the sun was shining brightly in the azure blue sky. It didn't get any more perfect than that. Until the other woman showed up. Zoë felt annoyed to have someone intrude into her paradise, but her annoyance turned to surprise when she realized the woman was the saleslady from A Wicca Good Time.

"What are you doing here?" she asked the long-haired woman.

The saleslady shook her head.

"Didn't I warn you?" she scolded Zoë.

"About what?"

"The Power of Three."

"Yeah, so?" Zoë shrugged.

The saleslady looked exasperated for a second, but she quickly regained her cool.

"Don't you realize that it is the reason you're here?"

"I don't get ya."

The saleslady counted to 10 before she spoke again.

"You caused the accident that put Toby's girlfriend into a coma, and now a similar accident has put you in the same situation."

"Oh." Zoë hadn't seen the connection. "But how is what happened to me three times worse than what happened to that tramp?"

"It wasn't."

"So, it is just mumbo-jumbo!" Zoë smiled triumphantly.

"No, it isn't," the saleslady scowled. "It just isn't finished with you yet."

"Oh," Zoë deflated. "So what's going to happen to me then?"

"I don't know. It all depends on what happens to me."

"Why you?" asked Zoë, confused.

It was the saleslady's turned to be surprised.

"Didn't you know?" she asked.

"Know what?"

"I'm Toby's girlfriend. You can call me Shanra." She held out her hand for Zoë to shake, but her vengeful rival did not take it.

"You're his girlfriend?"

"Yes."

"And you're a witch?"

"Yes."

"And whatever happens to you while you're in a coma is going to happen to me, only much, much worse?"

"Yes."

"So, I'm totally rooked?"

Shanra smiled.

"Totally," she answered before she faded away from sight.

🕷 🕷 🕷

Toby awoke on a spare bed in the hospital. Still feeling dizzy, he walked back to the room that held both his former and current girlfriends. But before he could walk in on them, a crew of doctors and nurses flew past him. Too busy to notice him, they didn't say anything when he followed them into the room. Shanra was flat lining and they were there to try to resuscitate her.

Toby was too stunned to react and observed the drama in front of him as if it was a scene from a dramatic television show. Orders he didn't understand were shouted out and those scary electric paddles were placed on Shanra's chest. The doctors used them several times until the sound of Shanra's heart beating was heard in the beeps of the machine she was connected to. Toby cried with relief, but this feeling was quickly extinguished when Zoë began to flat line. It took a second for the shocked crew to react, but once they did the whole procedure was repeated. It took them longer and they had to fight much harder, but finally they were able to get Zoë's heart started again.

They made Toby wait in the lobby for a couple of hours after that, but then a nurse approached him and told him that Shanra was awake. He ran to the room and wept when he saw her conscious and lucid in her bed.

"You had me so scared," he told her.

"Sorry about that," she whispered to him, her voice hoarse and tired.

Toby looked over to the other bed.

"You're not going to believe—" he started.

"She's your ex," Shanra interrupted.

"How did you know?"

"I have my ways. It's too bad about her, though."

"Why? What happened?"

Shanra looked around to see that no one could hear her.

"They thought I was still unconscious when they talked about it, but I heard it all. They screwed up when they revived her. The bottle that had the adrenalin they shot into her was mislabeled and it really contained some drug with one of those long unpronounceable names. They have no idea how it could have happened, the chances are like a million to one."

"Is she going to be all right?"

"No. Apparently the drug is meant to be used only on violent mental patients. They use it instead of surgery."

"What kind of surgery?"

"Lobotomies."

If she had been able to form a single thought, Zoë probably still would have reeled at the idea that the Power of Three had made sure her crime against Shanra hadn't gone unpunished. It ensured that, like her rival, she was brought to the brink of death by peanut butter. It then ensured that when she was pushed over that brink, a team of doctors would be there to bring her back. It also ensured that among them there would be a mislabeled vial that inexplicably contained a drug that the hospital didn't even keep in stock. And, finally, it ensured—after Toby had gone home and Shanra had been moved out of the critical ward—that she woke up.

When her eyes opened she felt different, but she couldn't tell how. A stream of drool began to flow out of her mouth, but she felt no impulse to wipe it away. She didn't feel much of anything. It took all her concentration just to stare at the wall in front of her. It didn't even occur to her that she no longer remembered her own name or that she loved a man named Toby or that—when it comes to magic—the universe has a way to make sure a person does only good.

A Castle on a Mountain

"Is this where I sign?" Lionel asked his business manager, Clive, as he pointed to the part of the contract that read "Signature." Clive nodded and—with a single pen stroke—Lionel spent four million American dollars.

"I own a castle," he smiled, having fulfilled the last of his childhood dreams.

Growing up in a housing project in Manchester, England, Lionel always knew that he would become a rock star. But unlike his friends, who shared similar fantasies, he alone had what it took to make his dream come true. When he was 17 he changed his name to Rash Radly and formed a punk rock band called The Visigoths. They did pretty well for a few years, but it was when he left them to go solo that he became a superstar thanks to his hit song "You Can Burn Our Love Down (I'll Just Build It Back Up)."

Over the next 10 years he toured, released more hit records and made more money in six months than the rest of his family did in their combined lifetimes. When the decade ended, he was tired. He had been on top of the charts longer than he had any right to and it was obvious to him that his brand of rock music was soon to become passé, so he did what so many of his fellow superstars refused to do—he retired while he still mattered.

The problem was that he had no place to retire to. During all his years on tour, he had lived in one hotel room after another and had never thought to buy a house in one particular spot to settle down. However, when it came time for him to find a place to live, he knew exactly

what he wanted. Unfortunately there weren't as many cas-
tles available for sale as he had assumed. Many were considered important historical sites and were protected by
their governments, others were owned by aristocratic
families whose titles went back 1000 years or more and
almost all of the rest were in such disrepair it would
require a fortune even he didn't have to rebuild them.

This left him with few options, and by far the best of
the lot was Brownvig Castle, on a small mountain beside
the village of Draseul in the tiny country of Baristoran. It
was in perfect condition and was owned by a government
that was so strapped for cash there was nothing in the
country they wouldn't consider selling, including their
own citizens.

Left with just a few tour commitments to fulfill before
he could move in, he sent over a crew of designers and
architects to make his new home as comfortable as possible for when he arrived. Feeling an excitement he had
forgotten was even possible, he found it difficult not to
become impatient as the weeks passed and his final
farewell tour continued. Except for when he was asleep or
onstage, he was in constant contact with the crew at his
castle. When the tour finally ended he went to Baristoran
in a private jet, which was the only way to get there by air
since the small country had no airport and had only one
runway safe enough for an airplane to land on. Once he
arrived, just before midnight, he sat impatiently in the
back of a very old town car as it drove over the worst
public road he had ever been on. His castle was a three-
hour drive away and he tried to contact the crew at his
castle during the bumpy ride, but his cell phone wouldn't

work in a country that had started to use landlines only 20 years earlier.

Refusing to take "no service" for an answer, he dialed the number to the castle over and over again. He stopped only when he heard his driver curse right before the car hit something.

"What was that?" he asked the driver as the car skidded to a halt.

The driver said nothing and cautiously slid out of the vehicle. He checked to make sure the car was okay, and when he was certain that it was, he got back in and started to drive away.

"What did we hit?" Lionel asked again as the car began to move forward. "Don't ignore me. I know you can speak English."

"I didn't see what it was," the driver insisted, though Lionel could tell he was lying.

He turned around to look out the car's back window. The moon was shining brightly and he could see something on the road. Even though the car was rapidly moving away from it, he could tell that it was the figure of a person.

"Stop," he ordered the driver. "You hit somebody! We have to get them to a hospital!"

The driver refused to stop.

"Listen to me! As the person paying you to drive me across this bloody country I demand that you stop and help that person!"

"That was not a person," the driver insisted coldly.

"What are you talking about?"

The car skidded to another halt as the driver slammed on the brakes.

"Look out and see," said the driver.

Lionel turned to look out the car's back window and saw nothing. He squinted out into the distance and saw that the road was empty as far as his eyes could see.

"That was not a person," repeated the driver.

"Then what was it?" asked Lionel.

The driver stayed silent and turned back to the wheel to continue driving.

"What was it?" Lionel demanded to know.

"Not a person" was all his driver was willing to say.

Lionel stayed quiet for the rest of the drive while he tried to figure out what was going on. Every now and then he would look out one of the backseat side windows and catch a glimpse of a cabin or a small farm. From what he could see Baristoran was like some place out of an old black-and-white horror movie. It seemed like a place where villagers would gather together with torches at night to chase some poor misunderstood monster, proving them to be the real villains.

He tried using his cell phone a couple of more times before he gave up, hoping that the crew hadn't made any important decisions without his approval. His worries vanished, though, when he looked out the window to his right and spotted a sign which read "Draseul, Pop: 1200." Knowing that he was just a few minutes away from finally seeing his castle in person, he started to shift around in his seat like an impatient, excited five year old.

Just past three o'clock in the morning, the village was asleep, and its long main street was empty of any signs of life. That was why he was surprised when the driver stopped the car suddenly.

"This is as far as I go," the driver explained to him.

"But we're almost there," he protested.

"I go no further," the driver insisted. "Someone in the village will take you to Brownvig."

"But everyone's asleep! It'll be hours before they're up," Lionel tried to argue, but the driver refused to budge. Finally he got out of the car and the driver made a quick U-turn and drove away as fast as the old car could manage.

His luggage had already been sent to the castle with some supplies the crew had needed, so all he had with him as he waited on the dark main street was a useless cell phone and the clothes he was wearing. His annoyance eased slightly when he turned around and saw a beautiful mountain in the distance and the huge stone building that sat upon it.

"That's my house," he spoke aloud to himself, awed by what he saw.

Feeling tired, he sat down on the lawn in front of someone's home and stared at his castle. He yawned and hoped that the people of Draseul were early risers. And just as this thought popped into his head he saw someone walking on the road in the distance. It was a woman. Her clothes were very old and torn with age, which was odd because she was obviously quite young. She had the longest hair he had ever seen; it literally dragged on the ground as she walked. There was a strange look on her face, one of awe and wonder, as if she were seeing the

world for the first time. Curious, and hoping she could help him, he stood up and walked over to her. She seemed surprised to see him but didn't look at all afraid.

"Hello," he greeted her as he approached. "Do you speak any English?"

She nodded her head.

"Little," she told him. Her accent was very heavy, but she didn't sound as if she was from Baristoran.

Seeing her up close he was shocked by how pale she was. Her skin practically glowed it was so white. The only color she had was in her dark hair and her lips, which were so red they looked as though they had been soaked in blood.

"I'm trying to get to Brownvig," he pointed. "The castle? Do you know someone who can take me there?"

She smiled and shook her head.

"I know no one here," she explained to him. "Not anymore."

"That's too bad," he sympathized.

She just smiled at him. He was shocked to discover then just how beautiful she was. He stood quietly as she raised her hand and gently placed it on his face.

"You look so good," she told him. "But," she moved her hand away, "there is no time. Maybe some other day."

"Maybe," he agreed, even though he had no idea what she was talking about.

With that she moved past him and started walking down the road. He watched her, ignoring his beautiful castle behind him, until she faded out of sight. An hour later the sun rose and the village started to wake. Several people peeked out their windows to check out the stranger in their midst. Finally an older man saw him and grew excited. Still dressed in his bathrobe, the man ran out of his house with a big grin on his face.

"Rash Radly!" he greeted Lionel with a long handshake.

"That's me," Lionel smiled.

"I am Egorin, the mayor of Draseul. I have been expecting you."

"Really? That's good to hear."

"Give me a moment and I will get dressed and take you to your castle."

Lionel was impressed by how fast the old mayor could get dressed, because not two minutes later they were getting into a creaky old horse carriage to make the journey up to Brownvig. Pulling them were two young strong horses that didn't seem too happy about where they were heading. Egorin, who spoke excellent English, cursed them for their hesitation and shouted at them to go forward, which they eventually did without enthusiasm.

"So tell me, Rash," Egorin chatted as they moved toward the mountain, "what have you heard about the history of Brownvig Castle?"

Lionel thought about this for a moment before he realized he didn't know anything about his new home, which he admitted to his companion.

"Then I have much to tell you," said the old mayor before he shouted another curse at his two wary horses.

It was then that Lionel learned how Brownvig Castle had been built in 1507 by a rich French merchant named Baptiste who had become enthralled by the beauty of Baristoran when he went there to fulfill a business obligation.

"Baptiste did not come alone," Egorin explained. "He brought his daughter, Marianne, with him. Some say he built the castle to hide her away from all her suitors in France. She was very beautiful and it was thought that Baptiste did not want to see her taken away from him by a husband, but there were rumors that he had other reasons to move her to Baristoran."

"Like what?" asked Lionel.

"The usual foolish superstition," Egorin laughed with a dismissive wave. "The people here are very superstitious now, so you can imagine what they were like 500 years ago. They took one look at her and insisted she was cursed."

"Cursed?"

Egorin laughed again.

"It is silly I know. They said that she was not an ordinary woman, but a poor soul doomed by the curse of the Nosferatu."

"She was a vampire?" Lionel said, recognizing the term "Nosferatu" as the title of an old silent movie he had seen years before.

"So they said, but you must remember that back then being left-handed was enough to get you accused of being a witch. Chances are some silly girl in town was just jealous of Marianne's beauty and accused her of being in league with the devil. It would not have been the first time."

"So what happened to them? Were they attacked by a mob?"

"No," Egorin shook his head, "that only happens in old American movies. They lived in the castle for many years, but the rumors only grew as time went on."

"How come?"

"Well, some who saw Marianne insisted that she never seemed to get any older. Her father grew more aged and frail, but she looked the same as when she had first arrived. And then there were some villagers who insisted that often people would visit the castle and never be seen again. During the day that is. They claimed that these poor fools could be seen living in the forest at night, surviving on the blood of animals and any unfortunates who happened upon their path."

"Really?"

"Don't worry," Egorin smiled. "It is all fairy stories we tell to scare our children from playing in the forest. It is our version of what you call an urban legend."

"Then what happened to Baptiste and his daughter?"

"They grew old and died, like we all do eventually, and after they were gone no one else wanted to move into the castle because of all the silly superstition. So, there it has sat empty for nearly 500 years, until you decided to buy it."

For the next few minutes the two of them sat quietly, except for whenever Egorin was forced to shout a loud insult at the horses, and Lionel grew anxious as they approached the castle. When they were still a few minutes away, Egorin turned to him with a smile.

"Would you like to hear the other version of what happened during Baptiste's and Marianne's last days at Brownvig? The one the villagers tell?"

Lionel nodded and Egorin continued, obviously amused by the absurdity of the story he was about to share.

"They say that as Baptiste grew older, he had decided that he could not cure his daughter of her curse. He was afraid of what she might do once he was gone. He loved her too much to kill her, but he knew he had to make Baristoran safe from her cursed affliction."

"So what did he do?" asked Lionel.

Egorin started to laugh so hard he almost choked. His fit also managed to spook the horses even more. He allowed them to stop for a minute, as he told Lionel the rest of the story.

"They say that while she slept, he had his servants block her doorway and windows with mortar and bricks. When she woke she found herself imprisoned in her room. They say her screams for release could be heard far longer than any person could ever live without food or water, but eventually they stopped. Can you imagine anything more ludicrous than that? How could anybody believe that a father would entomb his daughter inside his own home? It is ridiculous."

With that he pulled on the horses' reins and shouted at them to get them moving again. Ten minutes later they were in front of the castle.

"It's even more beautiful up close than it is from far away," Lionel marveled as he climbed out of the carriage.

"Yes," Egorin agreed, "it is quite a sight."

"Thank you for the ride," said Lionel, "would you like to come in and see what my designers have done with the place?"

Egorin smiled and shook his head.

"I would like to," he said, "but though I do not believe in the silly legends about the castle, I would be lying if I said I wasn't wary of them. Some other day, perhaps."

"I'll hold you to that," Lionel smiled.

Egorin laughed and shouted at his horses to ride away, which they did eagerly, happy to be moving away from the castle.

Lionel turned toward the huge stone building and saw that one of its massive doors was slightly ajar, leaving just enough space for a person to pass through. He walked through it and shouted out to alert everyone of his presence.

"Sweetykins," he called, "Daddy's home!"

There was no response. He realized that it was still early in the morning and everyone was probably still asleep. He walked through the castle's courtyard, which his landscaper had turned into a lush garden with an ornate fountain and a path fashioned out of large marble stones. From there he entered the castle and was awed by the work his crew had done in the large open hall. But before he could admire it too much, he heard someone call out his name.

He turned and saw Hazel, his chief designer, an older woman in her 50s. She looked incredibly tired and frightened, her face was red from crying and her clothes were bloody and torn.

"What happened to you?" he asked as he ran over to her.

"It happened so fast," Hazel sobbed as Lionel sat her down in a nearby chair.

"What did?"

"Simon," she said, referring to the crew's construction manager and chief architect. "He discovered that based on the castle's dimensions, there had to be a room hidden between two of the walls in the southeast corner. Last night, he found out where it was and sent his men to tear down part of the wall so we could get into it."

Lionel turned white.

"There was someone in there, wasn't there?" he whispered to her softly.

Hazel nodded.

"We all came running when we heard the screams. She was…she was…" Hazel could hardly bring herself to say the words "feeding on them. Like an animal! We ran from her, but she chased us. I hid away in a closet, but I heard her when she captured Simon. She spoke to him. She had a French accent and she told him that she had been starving for the past five centuries and then she killed him."

Lionel felt sick as he recalled talking to the beautiful stranger he had come across walking down the road. She had told him that he looked so good to her, but there was no time. He now knew what she had meant. If the sun had not been about to rise within the hour, she would have sunk her fangs deeply into his neck.

"Did anybody else make it?" he asked her.

"No," she shook her head. "No one made it. Everyone is dead."

"We've got to get you to a doctor," he told her, "there has to be someone in the village."

"No," she shook her head once again, "you don't understand. It's too late. *Everyone is dead.* Including me."

Lionel jumped away from her.

"I can feel it inside me," she explained. "I've been dead for only a few hours and I can feel the hunger growing.

Imagine what that poor woman must have felt between those walls. Starving for 500 years."

Lionel turned and started to run, but he was stopped when someone threw his body into him. It was Simon.

"I'm sorry I have to do this to you, Rash," he apologized, "but a bloke's got to eat."

Lionel screamed as Simon sunk his teeth deeply into his neck. As he screamed, the men and women who worked to rebuild his castle came out from the shadows and watched. Within a minute Lionel was no longer conscious.

A few hours later, his eyes opened. He felt different. He felt cold. But most of all, he felt very hungry.

Under His Bed

There were two reasons no one sympathized with Josh when he insisted that a monster lived underneath his bed. The first was the obvious fact that monsters weren't real. The second was that, at the age of 34, Josh was far too old to harbor such a juvenile paranoid fantasy. Josh understood this. He wasn't a crazy person, so he was fully aware of how crazy he sounded when he explained his odd belief, but as far as he was concerned, that didn't stop it from being true.

Though he had never actually seen the monster, the clues pointing toward its existence were far too obvious to be ignored. First there were the strange rumbling noises that he heard at night, which sounded like an inhuman combination of heavy breathing and loud snoring. Then there was the fact that whenever he went to sleep with a half-eaten snack left on his bedside table, it would inevitably be gone the next morning. There also was the strange smell that lingered in the room, no matter how many bottles of vanilla-scented deodorizing spray he emptied into it. And finally there were the large footprints that could occasionally be found on the room's plush white carpeting. As far as he was concerned, the combination of all this evidence served as irrefutable proof of his—admittedly bizarre—theory.

His friends, coworkers and family, though, were not as easily convinced as he was. They had no problems whatsoever refuting the irrefutable and shot down the veracity of his clues one by one. First, they pointed out, the "inhuman" noises he described most likely came from his own body, as anybody who had ever lived or camped with Josh knew that the snores he created could easily be confused with the groans of a large animal. They then reminded him that he was also prone to sleepwalking, which would explain the missing food and strange footprints. When he asked them to account for the room's strong odor, they would usually become embarrassed before politely suggesting to him that it wouldn't hurt if he took a shower more often. They would also point out the fact that whenever anyone looked underneath his bed, the only thing to be found was a stray sock or a collection of dust balls.

Annoyed by their skepticism, Josh would impatiently inform them that the creature appeared only at night when he was alone in the room, which he admitted sounded a bit convenient, but was still true nonetheless. But, despite this logic, they refused to believe him. Finally their skepticism grew so irritating he decided he had to do something about it, but it took him quite some time to figure out just what that thing would be.

It finally came to him while he was doing some research on the Internet. It occurred to him that all he had to do to prove he was right was to connect a webcam to his computer, place it in his bedroom and set up a Web site where people could watch what happened in his room during the night. Possessed with the kind of energy that can come only from having a monumentally brilliant idea, Josh raced out of his house and purchased all the necessary equipment.

After a long week spent setting everything up, Josh was ready to go live coast-to-coast. He sent e-mail messages to everyone he knew, informing them of his project and telling them where to go online to watch him. Many of them e-mailed him back, and their response was unanimous. They thought he had lost his mind. Josh ignored them. He went into his room and turned on his camera. Out of curiosity he ran over to his computer and went to his Web site and was thrilled to see his bedroom broadcast to the world. He sat there for over an hour and watched as the camera documented the mind-numbing boredom of an empty room, hoping that at some point the monster would decide to stir. It didn't, and Josh's eyes grew heavy with sleep. With a long-drawn-out, arm-stretching yawn, he decided that it was time to go to bed.

He went to his room and started to undress, then realized that he wasn't sure he wanted his Internet audience to see him in the altogether. He grabbed his pajamas, walked over to his bathroom and changed there. He then went back to his room, waved goodnight to the camera and all those who were watching him, turned off the light and went to sleep.

No one bothered to log in and watch him sleep that night, and even if they had, all they would have seen was Josh tossing and turning in his bed before he got up and sleepwalked around the room for 10 minutes. Not once would they have caught even the slightest glimpse of an inhuman monster. Josh didn't see the monster, either, when he reviewed the eight hours of webcam footage he'd recorded. Disappointed, but still convinced he was on the right track, Josh theorized two possibilities for the monster's on-camera absence. Either the creature was camera shy, or it was invisible. He especially liked the latter theory, because it also explained why he had never seen the creature himself. He posted these two possible explanations on his Web site and received 11 e-mail messages from friends and family urging him to seek professional psychiatric help.

Josh became more and more convinced about these two theories as the months passed and his camera failed to catch a glimpse of the monster for even one second. But as strong as his convictions were, he did have moments of doubt. Maybe his friends and family were right, he sometimes caught himself wondering. Maybe there really wasn't a monster living under his bed. It was just after one of these moments that he had another brilliant idea. He ran out and bought a new camera that was capable of recording images in heat vision. Even if the monster was invisible, it still had to produce heat, and this new camera would be able to see it.

Unfortunately, the new camera also failed to capture anything out of the ordinary. Finally, after six months, Josh was forced to conclude that everyone else was right and he was wrong. There was no monster under his bed. Feeling stupid and silly, he removed the webcam from his room and dismantled his Web site. And although most people would be pleased to know that their room wasn't cursed with the presence of an evil supernatural creature, Josh became profoundly depressed. It wasn't much fun to be proved a fool.

He lived with this depression for two months. Then one night, as he lay in his bed, he smelled something funny in the air. It was the odor of smoke and burning plastic. In the dark he turned his head and saw that somehow the cord connected to his table lamp had started to smolder and burn. By the time he jumped out of bed, the cord had begun to burn in earnest and flames attacked his wooden nightstand. Out of instinct he ran out of his room and found the small fire extinguisher he kept under the sink in the kitchen. With it he ran back into his room, stood in front of the nightstand and sprayed a thick layer of foam onto the fire, extinguishing it. He then looked under his bed, and though he couldn't see any flames, he decided to give it a blast from the extinguisher just in case. As he sprayed the foam, he was shocked to hear a loud, inhuman scream. In front of his amazed eyes, the entire bed upended itself as if a very strong animal had thrown it up into the air. It was then that he saw the foam he had sprayed rise from the floor. As it did, he could see that it conformed to the invisible body that it covered.

It was at that moment that Josh began to shake. Not because he was terrified of the invisible foam-covered creature in front of him, but because he was so thrilled to realize that he had been right all along. No one had believed him, but every single one of his theories had been correct. Just as he wondered why the special camera he'd bought hadn't picked up this creature's heat signature, he discovered the reason when a huge foam-covered appendage reached out and gripped him by the throat. It was the same temperature as the room.

While most people in this situation would spend their last seconds screaming in horror as the entirety of their lives flashed in front of their eyes, the only thought in Josh's head as the monster sliced into him with long, sharp, invisible claws was that he regretted taking down the webcam and dismantling the Web site. If he had kept them just a few months longer, then everyone would have known that he had been right all along.

They All Laughed

Xandi had difficulty explaining to people why she liked her piercings so much, which was strange, since she had 37 of them and was asked the question almost every day. She liked the way they looked; she liked how they made her stand out in a crowd (assuming that the crowd wasn't at a punk rock concert or a tattoo shop) and she liked the way it felt when she got one. Most people couldn't understand that last part.

"But doesn't it hurt?" they would ask.

"Sure it does," she would answer, "but in a good way."

People thought she was nuts, and maybe she was, but there was something about the rush of adrenalin that she felt every time the needle pierced her skin that she found intoxicating. Unfortunately one of the drawbacks of being addicted to this particular rush was the way it limited her employment options. Most places that would jump at the opportunity to hire a girl as charming and attractive as she was refused to even give her an interview as soon they saw her walk through the door. Some potential employers even went so far as to insult her by laughing at her before saying, "We don't hire freaks" or "This isn't the circus, sweetie."

The situation was becoming so desperate that she was close to having to choose between keeping her beloved piercings and having a place to live and food to eat. Thankfully it didn't come to that. Through a friend she got a job at a private laboratory, taking care of the animals and cleaning up after the scientists.

At first she feared that the experiments she assisted with involved harming the animals, but fortunately she discovered that this wasn't the case. At the moment, the scientists in the lab she worked with were doing research on behavior, which meant the animals—in this case mice—were only expected to race through a maze or two and weren't infected with any horrible diseases or forced to ingest possibly toxic substances. She actually ended up enjoying the experience. For the most part the scientists left her alone, as they were too busy theorizing and filling out grant applications to be social, which meant she wasn't forced to spend endless hours talking about the weather and the latest reality TV shows as she would have at any other job. Instead she just went about the place with her earphones blasting the latest punk rock CD, tidying up and feeding the mice.

But, given the nature of the universe, the cooler the job got the more likely it was to end. Six months after she was hired, the scientists she was working with had their grants revoked and were kicked out of the space. The mice were sold and Xandi assumed she was out of a job until she learned that the group that was moving into the space was willing to keep her on as an assistant. She was grateful, although she was a bit concerned about what she would be assisting with.

Three weeks into her time with them, she still didn't know. As an assistant she was just expected to keep the place clean and fetch things. She didn't understand the purpose of the experiments that were being done, and no one ever bothered to explain them to her. The entire group comprised three scientists, all of whom struck

Xandi as being insane. It got to the point that if she had ever caught one of them rubbing his hands together while proclaiming "They all thought me mad, but I'll show them! I'll show them when I *rule the world! Bwa-ha-ha-ha!*" she wouldn't have been the least bit surprised.

It turned out that Xandi was a remarkably good judge of character.

The three scientists she worked for, Dr. Olaf Guttmonson, Dr. Hortz Zeifly and Dr. Jon E. Smith, were all bitter outcasts from top-secret government programs and they had come together out of a shared desire to pool their demented knowledge and use it to take over the planet. Fortunately for the world, they spent far too much time bickering among themselves to dominate the lab, much less anywhere else.

Their goal was to create a genetically perfect super soldier, and to this end they were laboriously constructing a DNA sequence that would take humanity and move it significantly up the evolutionary ladder. This new human would be smarter and faster, require less food and no sleep, be able to withstand extreme temperatures and be significantly stronger than anyone who had ever lived before. They were nearly finished, but they had yet to figure out a way to allow for all these attributes but still create a person who would obey their commands and follow orders without question. They spent months trying to find a gene for what was essentially a learned behavior.

Xandi was completely oblivious to the true nature of their work, but she did find the experiments they performed to be getting stranger and stranger by the day. One morning they brought in a group of men and women dressed in flowing robes. Xandi could tell by the way they talked and the glazed look of happiness in their eyes that they were members of some kind of cult. They all sat together in a circle in the middle of the lab and started to chant, while the three scientists studied their every move.

This was just too much for her to take, so she did something she had never done before—she asked Dr. Smith what they were doing. He was so busy watching the cult members he didn't even look at her when he gave her an answer.

"We need to harness that," he explained.

Xandi assumed that the doctor was talking about some kind of mystical energy that was being created by the chanting, but he was actually referring to the cultists' willingness to accept illogical beliefs without question. Feeling stupid for even asking, Xandi turned away and started cleaning up the experiment that the three doctors had performed the night before. Desperate, they had attempted to take a gene they had found that nurtured a rebellious attitude in a person and reverse it so it had the opposite effect. They knew it would never work, but figured at that point that it was worth a shot.

As the cultists chanted, Xandi lifted the cold steel tube, which contained the failed strand of DNA. It tingled against her skin. She had never felt such a thing before, so she put it down and then picked it up again, to see if it was just the result of static electricity. It still tingled. She turned to mention this to Dr. Smith when a bright light flashed in the room along with a near-deafening boom.

When Xandi awoke she was lying on a steel table. The three doctors stared down at her with looks of concern and amazement on their faces. The cult members appeared to be gone.

"She's alive," Dr. Guttmonson whispered to himself when he saw her eyes open.

"How do you feel?" asked Dr. Zeifly.

"Good," Xandi admitted. "Better than good. I feel great."

It was true—as she sat up on the table she felt better than she ever had before. Not only did she feel better, but she almost didn't recognize all the messages her senses were sending her. She took out her contacts and saw the world clearer than she ever had before. She listened for a second and heard sounds she had never previously heard. There were a thousand new smells in the air. She could feel tiny specks of dust as they floated in the air and touched her skin. In her mouth the taste of metal was overpowering, which she assumed was because of her tongue ring.

With her powerful new eyes she caught a glimpse of herself in a small mirror on the other side of the lab. She screamed, but more out of surprise than terror.

"What happened?" she asked the doctors.

"We cannot explain it," Dr. Zeifly admitted. "At least not scientifically."

"There was an explosion," Dr. Smith explained.

Xandi looked around, but she didn't see any damage.

Dr. Smith shook his head.

"It wasn't that kind of explosion."

"Then what was it?" she asked.

"We think it had something to do with the chanting. It caused a mystical force to appear inside the lab," suggested Dr. Guttmonson. "Though it makes no sense scientifically, it allows for the only hypothesis we can all agree upon."

She jumped off the table and ran to the mirror, getting there in a tenth of the time it normally would have taken her. She looked into it and marveled at the fusion of metal and flesh that was now her face.

"Your piercings," Dr. Smith explained as she touched them. "They melted during the explosion. Do they hurt?"

"No," said Xandi. "They feel wonderful. They're so...beautiful." Curious, she stuck out her tongue at her reflection and saw that her tongue ring had also melted, which explained the strong metallic taste in her mouth. She stared at herself for a long time until she finally turned and asked the doctors the obvious question. "What happened to me? Why do I feel so good? It can't just be the explosion."

The doctors explained almost everything to her, neglecting only to mention the reason behind their research and the agreement they had made while she had lain unconscious on the table. Wanting to take advantage of this fortunate opportunity, they had decided—if she exhibited signs of superhuman ability—to dissect her and learn how the transformation affected her inner organs.

But now that she was awake and obviously gifted with abilities beyond that of any normal person, they had no idea how they were going to get her into a position where they could kill her and cut her open to perform the autopsy. They couldn't sneak up on her with syringes filled with poison, because she could hear every move they made. They couldn't knock her unconscious with a blunt object, because she could move far faster than they could. They had no gases that her new improved lungs would be damaged by breathing in, and there was no chance that she was going to get tired and go to sleep.

As she continued to look in the mirror and marvel at her new appearance, the three men communicated through written notes, trying to figure out how to dispose of her.

"Why don't we just shoot her?" wrote Dr. Smith after all the other options were dismissed. The other two looked at him and shrugged. It wasn't elegant, but if they acted quickly enough, it would get the job done.

Dr. Zeifly kept her distracted as Dr. Guttmonson retrieved a revolver he kept in a locked drawer of his desk. A practiced shot, he crept slowly behind Xandi, trying not to sound suspicious. When he was just a few feet from her, she turned toward him, and—with the gun already raised—he pulled the trigger. The bullet hit her square in the forehead and she dropped to the ground like a brick. Dr. Zeifly grabbed her wrist and checked her pulse.

"That did the trick," he informed his compatriots. "Let's get her up on that table."

Twenty minutes later, Xandi's body was on the table and Dr. Smith was getting ready to open her ribcage. He paused when a voice interrupted his concentration.

"Do you mind?" asked Xandi, causing the three doctors to jump up at the same time. They turned toward her head and saw that the young woman was very much awake. Dr. Smith looked down into the inside of her body and saw that her heart was not beating.

"That's not possible!" he panicked. "You're dead!"

"Yeah? If I'm so dead, then how come I'm talking to you right now?" she asked him.

Finally realizing what was happening, Dr. Zeifly started to scream and ran away from the table. Dr. Guttmonson fainted and Dr. Smith just stood and stared in disbelief.

"It's not possible," he repeated to himself. "It goes against every principal of science."

Xandi pulled out all the medical instruments they had inserted into her and used her hands to close the crevice in her abdomen. Dr. Smith watched, stunned, as her skin closed up and healed in front of his eyes. There wasn't even a scar left to indicate that she had been cut open.

"You're forgetting what you all told me," she reminded him as she sat up on the table. "There was no scientific explanation for how this happened. It was a freak accident. And I'm the freak." She smiled. "And y'know what? I feel better now than I did before you guys shot me."

With that she hopped off the table and grabbed Dr. Smith by his throat. She easily lifted him off the ground with one hand. His feet dangled helplessly off the ground as he gasped for air. When he stopped struggling she threw him like a rag doll across the lab. His body crashed into the hard glass door of a supply cupboard, and blood began to seep on the floor as the shards cut into him.

Xandi looked down at the unconscious Dr. Guttmonson and bent down and snapped his neck as easily as if it were a fortune cookie. She then stood up straight and listened to the sounds that only she could hear invade the silence. She heard Dr. Zeifly running down the alley beside the lab. It took her less than half a minute to catch up with him. It took her less than 10 seconds to make sure he never ran—or did anything else—ever again.

Hearing sirens blare far off in the distance, she ran home, getting there faster running than it usually took her taking the bus. In her apartment the reality of her situation finally hit her. She was no longer human. She was no longer alive. With her face an exotic melding of metal and flesh, she now looked like no one else in the world. She had killed people as easily as if they had been ants underneath her feet.

Tears streamed down her face as she started to cry. She was so happy. This was the coolest thing that had ever happened to her. Little Xandi Safrow, the freak who had once been laughed at, was now the freak who was going to take over the world.

It felt so good that she could not help laughing.

"*Bwa-ha-ha-ha!*" her evil chortle echoed inside her metal-covered head as she began to formulate a wonderfully devious plan.

The Homecoming

Every Tuesday Elizabeth would leave her two young sons with a babysitter and take the bus to the poor side of town. Once there she would go into a filthy slum of an apartment building, walk up 10 flights of stairs and knock on a battered wooden door. A minute or two would pass and then the door would open and expose a tiny old woman in her late 80s, clad in a tattered gypsy dress with a colorful scarf tied around her head.

"Come in," the old woman would say to Elizabeth, her words coated with a heavy eastern European accent.

Elizabeth would walk inside the small apartment, which was stuffed to the ceiling with dusty bottles and books, take off her jacket and sit down at the small table in the center of the room. The gypsy woman would then walk slowly to a large cabinet in the corner, whose doors always creaked whenever she opened them. From out of it she would remove a large glass sphere, which rested atop a red velvet pillow. She would then place the sphere on the table and sit down in front of it.

Elizabeth knew by then that she was supposed to stay quiet, so she would just sit and wait for the woman to speak. For several long minutes the old woman would stare into the glass sphere as she chanted a series of words Elizabeth couldn't understand. At the end of her chant a light would flare inside the sphere, and Elizabeth would see it reflected in the woman's eyes. It was then that she would find out what she had come all this way to hear.

"I see Quincy," the old woman would tell her. Quincy was Elizabeth's husband, who was currently away at war, fighting with the army against the Nazis.

"How is he?" Elizabeth would ask.

"He is well, but he misses you and your children. He dreams of the day he can come home, and his dreams will be answered soon."

"So he will survive the war?"

"He will live long enough to bury you all," answered the woman.

While to some that might have sounded ominous, to Elizabeth it meant that Quincy would live a very long life.

Finished, the old woman would put her glass sphere away and Elizabeth would pay her two dollars. She would then go back home, pay the babysitter and put her twin sons, Archie and Homer, to bed.

This routine stayed the same for several months, until one week the gypsy woman saw something unusual in her glass sphere. She squinted at it, as if it were distant and out of focus.

"Your husband…" she said, then hesitated.

"Yes?" asked Elizabeth.

"He is coming home to you…in a matter of days."

Elizabeth's eyes lit up with joy.

"Days? Are you sure?" she asked excitedly.

The old woman nodded.

Armed with this knowledge, Elizabeth spent the next few days getting ready for Quincy's arrival. She cleaned the house, bought enough food to feed a king and got herself a fancy new haircut. When she got back from the beauty salon, she put Archie and Homer into the bathtub

so they would be nice and clean for their father. As the water from the tap filled the tub, they splashed each other and giggled as they made bubbles with the soap. Elizabeth turned away from them to take another look at her new hairdo and almost had a heart attack when she heard the doorbell ring.

"Quincy!" she shouted excitedly as she ran out of the bathroom and down the stairs toward the door. Unfortunately, she was still wearing the heels she had put on for her trip to the beauty salon. The shoes were not designed for running, and her left heel snapped off and caused her to lose her step. She tumbled headfirst down the stairs and landed on the floor with a neck-snapping thud. The doorbell rang again, but Elizabeth was far too dead to answer the door.

Eventually the salesman at the door assumed that no one was home, and he picked up his case and went on his way. A few days later, Elizabeth's teenage babysitter arrived at the house, assuming she was needed as she had been every Tuesday for the past several months. She was surprised to find that no one answered the doorbell, but the door was unlocked, so she let herself in. Clad in only sandals, her feet were soaked immediately by the water that covered the floor.

"Elizabeth?" she shouted out, confused by what she had found. She turned toward the stairs and gasped when she saw Elizabeth lying dead in the pool of water that was caused by the rivulets streaming slowly, but steadily, down the stairs. A sudden rush of terror took hold of her when she realized where the water had to be coming from.

"Archie! Homer!" she shouted as she ran up the slippery stairway. She turned into the bathroom and screamed with horror when she saw the two drowned children lying at the bottom of the overflowing bathtub.

She called the police, and it was they who contacted Quincy's army superiors. They gave him a leave of absence, and he left the front to go back home and attend the funerals. Though he did not know it, the fortune-teller had been right. He had come home within a matter of days, and he had lived long enough to bury both his wife and children. Overcome with grief, he returned to the war and in a moment of unrelenting sadness deliberately stepped on a land mine, hoping that he might see his loved ones again in the world of the great beyond.

A Father's Love

When Luke's parents informed him that he would be staying at his Uncle Frank's for a month while they went on a trip to Europe, he was more than a little unhappy about it. Despite his protests that he was—at 14—old enough to stay at home by himself, they could not be persuaded to change their minds.

Luke liked his Uncle Frank, who was a very funny and generous guy, but something else made him unhappy about staying at the man's house. The problem was that his uncle had a peculiar hobby that had creeped Luke out ever since he was a toddler. A huge film buff, Frank collected movie posters. Specifically he collected horror movie posters, each more disgusting and disturbing than the last. A brief glance at any of the house's many walls was enough to give Luke nightmares for a week. And the worst thing was that the most frightening of all the posters was located in the house's only spare bedroom, right where Luke would be sleeping.

It was for a movie that Luke had never heard of, called *Sammy*, and even though he had no idea what it was about, he had decided that—based solely on the poster—it had to be the scariest film ever made. As far as he could tell, the movie must have been about a strange mutant child named Sammy, as the poster depicted a small child-like figure with the most horribly deformed face Luke had ever seen. The snarling creature had four sunken black eyeballs, two in the usual spots and two higher up on its forehead. Instead of a nose there was just an empty hole in the middle of its face, and its mouth, which was full of razor sharp teeth, was found misplaced on its left cheek. Its skin was pale white and covered with big red sores and blisters, some of which oozed clear viscous fluids. Patches of dark hair covered the top of its head, along with random bald spots that exposed a dry and damaged scalp. Whenever he felt brave enough to look at it, Luke had trouble deciding if the image was the result of a photograph of the world's greatest makeup job or the most convincingly photo-realistic drawing he had ever seen.

The creature from *Sammy* quickly found its way into Luke's nightmares. Even worse, the poster was almost always the first thing he saw when he woke up from one of these horrible dreams. He wanted to ask his uncle to take it down, but he didn't. After having argued so long and hard with his parents that he was mature enough to take care of himself for the month, he knew that admitting a movie poster frightened him that badly would only prove to them that they had been right to make him stay with Frank. So as the days passed, he did his best to ignore the poster and rid his mind of the horrific image it had burned into his dreams.

He spent most days watching television, playing with his uncle's dog, Kaycee, or reading one of the hundreds of science fiction books his uncle owned. He actually didn't see much of his uncle, who worked long hours at the local power plant and who spent the bulk of his free time either watching movies or reading. But Luke soon noticed that two or three times a week, his uncle would spend a long time upstairs in the house's attic. Luke assumed that he went there to work on the kind of hobby that an older man might be too embarrassed to admit he still pursued, such as model building or baseball card collecting, so he didn't think it was too strange when his uncle changed the subject the only time Luke brought it up. He did wonder, though, what went on up there. But as curious as he was, he decided to try to respect his uncle's privacy.

There is, however, a huge difference between trying to do something and actually doing it. The problem for Luke was that imagining what his uncle did up there was a very good way to stop thinking about *Sammy* and all of the house's other posters, so he did it as much as he could, and the more he did it the more he wanted to learn the truth. The problem was that his uncle kept the attic door shut tight with the same kind of combination lock that Luke used for his locker at school. While there was no way for him to open the lock, he realized that the latch and bolt it went through could easily be removed with a screwdriver or—if the screws had been put in extra tight—an electric drill.

Armed with the necessary tools, Luke waited patiently for his uncle's car to pull out of the driveway and disappear down the road before he ran to the attic door and got to work. It turned out that a screwdriver couldn't get it done, so he picked up the cordless drill he found in his uncle's garage and searched through a small blue case full of drill bits for the one that he needed. A few minutes later the lock was off the door. Feeling a rush of excitement from his accomplishment, Luke turned the knob to open the door and was immediately disheartened when he discovered that it too was locked, and it required a key to be opened. Assuming that the key was on the road to the power plant with his uncle, Luke almost gave up right there, but then he looked at the drill still in his hand and at the door's exposed hinges. It occurred to him that it wouldn't be that hard to take the door off completely. He just hoped he could put it back on without doing anything to it that would arouse his uncle's suspicions.

The hinges proved to be a lot trickier to remove than the bolt and latch had been, but after a good hour of sweaty labor he was almost done, with just three more screws to go, when he was alarmed by the sound of the drill's motor. Instead of whirring powerfully, it started to whimper, until finally it lacked the strength required to turn the screws. The tool's rechargeable battery had been drained by the extended use and no longer had the power necessary to get the job done. More afraid that he wouldn't be able to get the door back on before his uncle got home than of not finding out what was in the attic, Luke began to panic. But before he could get too worked up he looked down at the drill and saw a small sticker attached to it. It read, "In case of low battery, either stop and recharge or continue with included A/C Adapter." He could keep going if he found the drill's detachable cord. It took him two hours of steady searching throughout the house, but eventually he found what he was looking for. His relief was quickly extinguished when he got back to the door and found that there was no outlet along the stairway to the attic to plug the adaptor into. He ran downstairs and discovered that the nearest available outlet was in the living room, which for his purposes might as well have been 100 miles away.

It was getting close to noon and virtually every appliance in the house, except for the fridge, was turned off as Luke looted the house for every extension cord and power bar he could find. In the end he needed two long cords and three bars in order to get close enough to the door to finish the job. Finally, after over four hours of work, he removed the door and walked into the dark attic.

Unlike the protagonists of the kinds of movies whose posters Uncle Frank collected, the first thing Luke did when he stepped inside was search for a light switch. There wasn't one by the door, so he was forced to creep along the wall until his hand found one 10 feet to the right. He flipped it on and was rewarded with the sight of a small dank space filled with a wide variety of old and badly damaged plastic toys, a small television and a large box-like object that was hidden underneath a ratty and tattered red blanket. Slowly, he walked toward this last item to see what exactly the blanket hid, but he stopped when he heard the phone ring downstairs. Uncle Frank always called him sometime around lunch, so Luke turned around and flew down the stairs to answer the phone before the machine picked it up, as he didn't want his uncle to think that anything was out of the ordinary.

"Hello?" he answered just in time, trying his best not to sound like he was out of breath.

"Heya kiddo," his uncle greeted him, "how are things going on the home front?"

"The usual," Luke lied, "same-old, same-old."

"That's good. It looks like I'm actually going to get home on time today, so I thought I'd pick up some food on the way. How does some chicken sound?"

Luke made some clucking noises, which made his uncle laugh.

"Maybe we'll get lucky and we'll get a bucket with a battered and fried rat in it, just like that story I told you a couple years ago," his uncle reminded him. "Do you remember that?"

"Yeah," answered Luke, neglecting to mention that he had refused to eat take-out chicken for four months after he had heard it.

"Anyway, I'll see you at dinnertime. Try not to do anything too exciting until then, okay."

"I won't."

They said goodbye to each other and hung up. As soon as he put the phone down, Luke realized he had just a few more minutes to explore the attic if he wanted to have enough time to make sure he covered all his tracks before his uncle got home. He ran up the stairs and into the dark room and tore the blanket off the hidden object, revealing a large rectangular cage and the heavy odor of a wild animal. He looked into the cage and found that it was empty, save for a blue blanket. He quickly began to panic when he realized that the animal that his uncle kept in the cage must have gotten out while he was on the phone. Not knowing what kind of animal it had been, he wasn't sure how wise it would be for him to go and search for it. The fact that his uncle was so secretive about its existence had to be proof that something wasn't normal about this particular pet, but he searched for it anyway. Unfortunately, it was nowhere in sight and as the minutes quickly evaporated, he was forced to give up the search and put the door back on its hinges.

It turned out to be quite a bit harder to put the door back on than it had been to take down. When he finally got it back up and finished putting the latch and bolt back on, he had just half an hour to put away all the extension cords and power bars he had pilfered throughout the house. This also meant he had to reset all the clocks and appliances he had unplugged. He briefly toyed with the idea of claiming they had all gone off during a local power failure, but he realized that—given where his uncle worked—this idea probably wouldn't play. There was just five minutes left to spare on the last clock he set, but he felt no relief. He had left several small—but noticeable—scratches on the attic door during the course of the day and—along with the missing animal—it was only a matter of time before his intrusion into his uncle's privacy was discovered. His worries were further compounded by the odd sounds he heard creak and rattle around him. Though he wanted to dismiss them as the kind of noises that could be heard in any quiet house, he feared that they were being made by something that definitely shouldn't be out and about.

Feeling guilty, tired and afraid, he flopped down nervously on the living room couch and turned on the TV and sat there until his uncle came home with a bucket of fried chicken 10 minutes later. The strange sounds continued to clatter throughout the house as the two of them sat down to eat, but luckily his uncle didn't seem to notice them. Luke's nerves had shrunk his appetite down to nothing, and it was all he could do to choke down a drumstick. After a few moments of uncomfortable silence at the table, he excused himself and went to his room, where the first thing he saw was that horrible poster. He lay down on his bed and closed his eyes and hoped that somehow everything would turn out all right.

His hopes were shattered when about an hour later he heard his uncle shout out with a voice full of disheartening anger.

"LUKE!" he roared. "What have you done!?"

Before Luke could get up from his bed, his door burst open and his uncle ran to him and grabbed him roughly by the shoulders.

"Tell me you didn't go into the attic!" he pleaded, and it was at that moment that Luke realized that it wasn't anger that he heard in his uncle's voice but the very worst kind of fear. "TELL ME!"

"I just wanted to know what you did up there," Luke admitted tearfully, frightened by his uncle's obvious terror. "I didn't mean to let whatever was in there out, but it got loose when I was talking to you on the phone."

"Did you see where he went?"

"I didn't see it at all. You called before I could remove the blanket and it was gone when I got back."

"So he could be anywhere."

"I guess..." said Luke before he asked the big question. "What is it, Uncle Frank? Why are you so scared of it?"

Uncle Frank looked at Luke for a second before he buried his face into his hands. He stayed like that for a long time before he lifted his head and started to speak.

"Luke," he said, "how much do you know about your Auntie Maureen?"

Luke answered by saying that all he knew about her was that she had been Uncle Frank's wife who, along with their only son, had died during childbirth a couple of years before Luke was born.

His uncle nodded his head slowly at this and sighed heavily before he told Luke a secret no one else in his family had ever been told before.

"Your aunt did die giving birth, that's a fact, but it wasn't from unstoppable hemorrhaging like her doctor and I told everyone. No, she was murdered. Murdered right in front of us by the child she had carried. That's a horrible thing for a father to say about his son, but I was there and I saw it. Just seconds after he took in his first breath he killed his own mother."

"But how?" Luke didn't understand.

"He was a monster, or as close as a human being could ever get to being one. Both physically and spiritually. It was all we could do not to kill him right then and there. By every law we had that right, but we didn't. He was my son, after all. We told everyone that he died with his mother and I took him home and raised him as best I could. This used to be his room, but then he got too big to manage and I had no choice but to keep him in the cage." He paused for a second as he thought about this. "You can't imagine how agonizing it feels to know that were it not for a collection of metal bars, your own son would happily tear into your neck."

"But how could anyone be that horrible?" asked Luke.

"I don't know," his uncle admitted. "All I know is that despite the evil malevolence that was always there in his eyes, I still loved him. I even put a picture of him up on the wall of his old room. I hoped it would make him seem even the slightest bit normal, but I had to disguise it as a poster for a horror movie and then—to explain why I would frame such a horrible thing—I had to collect real posters to surround it."

Luke turned pale when he heard this. He did not have to be told which poster his uncle was talking about.

"*Sammy*?" his voice shook as he whispered its name aloud.

His uncle nodded.

"What's he going to do?" asked Luke.

His uncle shrugged. "What would you do if someone had kept you inside a cage for almost a decade? He's going to do what he has wanted to do ever since he was born. He's going to kill me."

"We've got to call the police! They can find him and stop him," Luke insisted.

"No," his uncle shook his head, "they'll kill him. They'll have to. It's the only way they'll be able to stop him."

"But—"

"He's my *son*, Luke. I can't let him die like that. No, all I can do is wait for him." He pulled out his wallet and handed it over to Luke. "I want you to walk over to the payphone at the convenience store down the block and call a cab to take you home. There should be enough there to pay for the ride and anything you'll need before your parents get back."

"But—"

"GO!" his uncle shouted. "NOW!"

Terrified, Luke jumped up and ran out of the house and all the way to the store. When he got there he dialed 911 and begged the emergency operator to send over the police right away. Ten minutes later a squad car met him in the store's parking lot.

"It's my uncle," Luke explained, "his son is going to kill him! You have to hurry!"

The two officers raced to the house, and Luke ran as fast as he could behind their car. He watched as the two men entered the house with their guns drawn, and his heart pounded as he waited outside.

From inside the house a thundering wave of gunshots destroyed the neighborhood's silence. Luke watched as a small, pale and bent-over figure ran out the front door with a speed that didn't seem human. The two officers followed after it, but it was out of sight by the time they reached the sidewalk. One of the officers ran to the squad car and started shouting instructions into its radio.

"We need an ambulance and all available officers must be on the lookout for a...a..." he struggled to find the right words to describe what he had just seen, "a large white animal that appears to be some kind of primate. It kind of looks like a man."

Luke ran up to the other officer, who looked frightened and was out of breath.

"Is my uncle okay?" he asked.

The officer looked down at Luke and started to shake his head with disbelief.

"We went in there and saw him backed into a corner by that...that...*thing*. It was going to kill him, but when we aimed at it, he threw it out of the way and took the bullets himself." The officer's eyes were glazed with disbelief. "Why would he do that?"

Luke began to shake as he was overcome with tears. Through his sobs he tried to answer the officer's question, but he wasn't sure if he understood the truth himself.

Death's Best Friend

It all started when Jimmy accidentally electrocuted himself. It was early in the morning and he had yet to feel the effects of his first cup of coffee. His eyes still blurry from sleep, he had slid a couple of pieces of bread into the toaster and waited for them to pop up, all warm and toasty brown. He turned the radio on and just happened to catch his favorite epic rock song as it was beginning. The music woke him up, and he started to play air guitar as he sang. He got so involved in the music that he forgot about the toast, which had become stuck inside the toaster and started to burn. It was only when the smoke detector began to beep that he realized something was wrong. He turned around and saw that the smoke was coming from the slots of his toaster, so he instinctively grabbed a fork from the sink and stuck it into the slot to dig out the toast.

The electricity that surged through his body was enough to stop his heart. He landed on the ground with a thud and lay there until a bony hand bade him to get up. Stunned, he sat up and saw a very tall and skinny figure in front of him. The creature was dressed in a long black cloak, had no skin on its body and was holding a sharp farming implement.

"Dude!" Jimmy greeted him. "You're the Grim Reaper!"

"That's right," answered the Reaper, his voice a hollow gravelly sound that seemed to echo from his chest.

"Cool! Does that mean that I'm dead?"

"Yes," the ominous creature intoned solemnly.

"Well, that bites," Jimmy complained, "but I guess it couldn't be helped, huh? I'm only 25, but when it's your time to go, it's time to go."

"That's correct."

"Cool. So where are we going?"

"I am taking you to the land of judgment where your soul shall be—" the Reaper was interrupted by an annoying beeping noise.

"What's that?" asked Jimmy.

The Reaper sighed.

"It's my cell phone," he admitted. "Give me a second."

From his dark cloak the Reaper pulled out a small cell phone and then spoke into it.

"Reaper here," he answered. A few seconds passed as the person on the other line asked him a question. "Yes," said the Reaper, "I've got him right here. I was just about to take him to the judgment place...Really? Are you sure?...Did Bennie screw up the paperwork again?...Can't we replace him?...I know, it just makes me look bad...Yeah, I know, it's not your fault...Don't worry, I'll take care of this. Tell Suzie I said 'Hi.'"

He hung up. Even though he had no skin, Jimmy could still tell that the summoner of souls before him was blushing with embarrassment.

"It looks like a mistake has been made," the Reaper explained sheepishly. "You're not due to face your judgment just yet."

"Really? Does that mean I'm not dead?"

"That's correct," the Reaper nodded.

"Cool," Jimmy grinned. "I didn't want to be a bring-down, but I was kinda bummed about my—y'know—shuffling off this mortal coil. I figured I'd get another 10 or 20 years at least."

Somehow, without lips, the Reaper smiled. "Try 50," he suggested.

"Fifty!" Jimmy repeated excitedly.

Realizing what he had said, all the color that shouldn't have been in the Reaper's face in the first place immediately drained out of it. "I shouldn't have told you that," he said to Jimmy. "No one is supposed to know how long they have. It's against the rules. My boss would kill me if he found out."

"Don't worry about it," Jimmy said reassuringly. "I won't tell."

"You promise?" asked the Reaper.

"Sure," Jimmy smiled. "It can be our little secret."

"Thanks," the Reaper said, breathing out with relief. "My butt was on the line there."

"So I really have 50 years before I'm supposed to die?" asked Jimmy.

The Reaper nodded.

"Do you want the date?" he asked.

Jimmy thought about it for a second and shook his head.

"Surprise me," he told the Reaper.

"Will do," the Reaper smiled. "I'll see you in 50, then."

"Yeah, see ya."

The Reaper vanished, and Jimmy awoke with a start. The smoke detector was still beeping and the toaster was now on fire. Feeling more energetic than he ever had before, he jumped up and put the fire out by throwing a wet dishtowel on it. He then turned off the smoke detector and threw away the blackened toast. Having just faced death, he felt incredibly alive. There were things he had to do.

The first item on his list was to fulfill a dream he had had for several years, ever since he had become a regular at the pub down the street. It was his favorite place in the world, and he would have considered it perfect were it not for the unwelcome presence of a lout named Chad Mayhew. Standing 6'6" and weighing over 300 pounds, Chad was the type of guy who liked to throw his considerable weight around to bully people to get what he wanted. He often harassed the other customers, started fights and even stole people's drinks in front of their faces, daring them with a look to do something about it. Jimmy had long wanted to stand up to Chad, but his natural survival instinct always stopped him. But now that he knew he was guaranteed 50 more years of life, he decided it was time to take his shot.

That night he walked into the pub and headed directly over to Chad, who, along with some friends, had just forced a group of people out of the booth they had been sitting in.

"Hey!" he shouted at Chad. The pub became instantly silent.

"Are you talking to me?" asked Chad incredulously.

"Yeah," answered Jimmy.

Chad stood up. He was a full foot taller than Jimmy. The rest of the patrons stared with horror as they anticipated the violence they were sure was to follow.

"Hey what?" asked Chad menacingly.

Jimmy hadn't thought of an answer for that particular question, so he took a second to figure out how to properly phrase his thoughts.

"Hey, you're easily the stupidest example of a dimwitted Neanderthal moron I've ever had the misfortune to meet. You're ugly, too. Big, stupid and ugly, that about sums it up."

Everyone in the pub gasped. The more sensitive patrons shielded their eyes to avoid witnessing the inevitable violence that was sure to follow such an insult.

Chad couldn't believe what he had been told. No one had ever insulted him like that in all his life. "Did you just call me stupid and ugly?" he asked Jimmy, bewildered.

"You smell bad, too," Jimmy answered him.

Luckily Jimmy didn't feel much of the pummeling he received from Chad, as he was knocked unconscious by the first punch. However, the enraged brute still pounded him until he was unrecognizable.

Bloody and battered, Jimmy opened his eyes and saw that everyone around him had frozen in time. An annoyed Reaper stood over him.

"What do you think you're doing?" asked the grim one.

"Hey man," Jimmy grinned, "nice to see you again so soon."

"I asked you a question."

"I just wanted to let this jerk know what everyone thought about him," answered Jimmy.

"And for that you were willing to nearly get beaten to death?"

"Well, sure it sounds crazy when you put it like that," Jimmy admitted, "but it seemed like a pretty good idea at the time."

"Does this have anything to do with your knowing how long you have to live?"

"A little, I guess."

The Reaper sighed.

"Jimmy, just because you know you've got a long time left to live doesn't mean you should put yourself in dangerous situations. You could get crippled or put into a permanent coma. As it is, you're going to need extensive plastic surgery just to rebuild your face."

"It was worth it," Jimmy smiled.

The Reaper groaned. He could tell by the look on Jimmy's broken face that he was going to see a lot more of this kid. Thanks to a quick slip of his tongue, he had turned the friendly young man into someone who no longer feared death, which meant there was no telling how much trouble he was going to get into in the future.

Almost as if by a miracle, Jimmy awoke inside the ambulance just as the paramedics were about to pronounce him DOA. His face had suffered such a mauling the emergency room nurse almost fainted when she saw him. The doctors were astounded he was still alive. He stayed in the hospital for several months as he underwent reconstructive facial surgery. Even the surgeons who performed the operations were shocked by how well they turned out. Somehow, Jimmy managed to look even better than he had before.

As for Chad, he was sentenced to six years in prison for assault. The day before he was scheduled for his release, he met the Reaper himself when he was shanked by another con for failing to return a borrowed copy of *Martha Stewart Living*. His friends were banned from the pub, and it became the ideal hangout Jimmy always believed it should have been.

Just as the Reaper feared, Jimmy wasted no time risking his life numerous different ways after he got out of the hospital. He rescued people from burning buildings. He went skydiving and took up rock-climbing. He organized a union at the company he worked for. He played rugby. He walked down dark alleys in bad neighborhoods late at night. He drove one of those SUVs whose tires were always exploding, causing the vehicle to flip over. He ate shellfish and nuts, despite lifelong allergies to both. He even once stopped a bank robbery in progress and took a bullet in the chest for his effort.

He eventually became recognized by the world records people as the man with the most near-death experiences. And every time he had one he would get a lecture from an aggravated Reaper.

"One of these days I'm just going to stop coming," the personification of death threatened him. "It wouldn't be so funny then, would it? And what happens if next time you end up with a body so mangled the doctors can't fix it? Just because you've been this lucky this far, doesn't mean your luck can't end."

Jimmy had heard this lecture before.

"Admit it, you'd miss me," he grinned at the Reaper.

"Ha!" laughed the Reaper derisively.

"Yeah, you'd miss me."

Jimmy was right, though the Reaper would never admit it. As the years passed, his lectures about the foolishness of Jimmy's actions became less about his being annoyed than about his genuine concern. Because of the very nature of his work, the Reaper got to meet literally every person who ever lived, but almost always only once or—in rare cases—twice. And about 90 percent of the time people weren't too keen to talk to him, as they were usually grumpy about having just died or nervous about what would happen to them in the judgment place. Jimmy was one of the only people he had gotten to know in the entire time he'd had the job, and he liked the guy. Sure, he wasn't the brightest bulb in the pack, but he always meant well. He admired how Jimmy had used his knowledge about the time he had left in the physical world to help people and not for his own benefit. It had occurred to the Reaper the last time they had gotten together—when Jimmy had a heart attack while running a marathon for charity—that Jimmy was his best and only friend. This made him feel sad, because he knew that eventually—on a day Jimmy would never expect—he would not be able to return his friend to the living realm.

But the Reaper didn't have a lot of time to dwell on this fact, as he was getting busier and busier as the years passed by. Even though people around the world were living longer and longer, there were still more dead people than there ever had been before. He would be working himself to the bone, if he hadn't already started out that way. The few minutes he spent with Jimmy every year or so amounted to the only vacation time he got. Despite his immortality, the effort was beginning to wear him out. He kept complaining to his bosses, but red tape always kept them from finding a workable solution. Plus, none of the agencies would work together, so even if his bosses got the weather people to ease up on the earthquakes, typhoons, hurricanes and other disasters, the nature people would introduce another disease and keep him just as busy.

Jimmy didn't work nearly as hard as his buddy. Thanks to a handful of extremely lucrative insurance claims, he never had to work again and spent his remaining years relaxing and doing what he could to help others. Despite all his near-death experiences, he remained healthy and looked at least a decade younger than his actual age. Knowing it was time to quit the daredevil stuff, he decided to make a difference by working as a volunteer at a hospice for terminally ill people. There he did his best to teach the dying that his friend the Reaper was really a cool guy and that they shouldn't be afraid of him.

The Reaper learned about his friend's efforts when he noticed that many of the people he picked up from the hospice mentioned that they had heard good things about him from an older man who always had a smile on his face. That Jimmy would do this for him moved him more than he could ever say. It also gave him an idea.

The final decade of Jimmy's life passed as if it really had been just a jubilant long weekend. Though he and the Reaper did not meet during that time, they had thought about each other constantly, and when Jimmy turned 75 he looked forward to seeing his friend for the last time. He now kind of regretted not asking for the date of his death, because not knowing made him slightly anxious. He was thinking about it one morning when he stepped into his shower. As he started lathering up a piece of soap, it slipped out of his hands. As he bent down to pick it up, he stepped on it and slipped.

When he woke up, his friend was standing above him.

"Hi," Jimmy smiled, slightly embarrassed to be caught naked.

"Hi Jimmy," the Reaper smiled back. "It's really good to see you again."

"Thanks."

"I mean it."

"I know you do," Jimmy said as he stood up. "Now, am I right in guessing this is the last time we'll ever meet?"

"No," the Reaper grinned.

Jimmy looked confused.

"You mean it's not my time? I'm early?"

The Reaper shook his head.

"No. Today is the day you die."

"But doesn't that mean I'm supposed to go to the judgment place? Aren't I supposed to never see you again after that?"

"That is how it usually works," the Reaper nodded.

"Then what's going on?"

"I have a proposal for you, Jimmy."

"What?"

"For thousands of years I've done my job alone, but I think it is time for that to change. I've talked to my superiors and they've agreed with me."

"I don't understand. Are you..." Jimmy paused. "Are you asking me to be your assistant?"

"No," the Reaper shook his head. "I'm asking you to be my partner."

Jimmy stared at the tall, cloaked skeletal figure in front of him.

"Would I have to look like that?" he asked with a doubtful expression.

"No. You can look however you want to look."

Jimmy laughed.

"You mean you actually *chose* to look like that?"

The Reaper frowned. "It's what I'm used to," he explained.

"I'm just teasing you," Jimmy said, grinning. "What would I have to do?"

"What I do and nothing more."

"Would we get to hang out together?"

"I'm certain of it."

Jimmy stood silent as he mulled all this over. "Okay," he decided. "I'll do it."

From that day anyone who died had an equal chance of being met by a tall skeleton in a black cloak holding a scythe or a short old man with a cheerful grin and a chipper attitude. While most people would have chosen to be taken away by the less frightening of the two, those who were taken by the Reaper were often surprised that—seeing him in person—they would never describe him as being grim.

The Red Dress

Natalie thought it was the most beautiful dress in the world. Tears came to her eyes as she lifted it out of its box and admired it at arm's length. It was a long, elegantly unadorned, bare-shouldered red dress, held up by thin, but sturdy, scarlet spaghetti straps. It was made out of the softest silk she had ever felt, and it looked like something worn by the most glamorous of movie stars and super-models. She could not believe that it was going to be her prom dress.

"So do you like it?" asked her father, who had given it to her.

"I love it!" she exclaimed tearfully. She put it down and gave him a big hug. "It's just wonderful! Thank you."

"You're welcome," he smiled.

"Why don't you try it on and see if it fits?" suggested her mother.

This sounded like the best idea Natalie had ever heard, so she rushed upstairs, ran into her bedroom and put it on. When she came back down, both of her parents were stunned speechless. Like all parents of daughters, they had believed that their child was one of the prettiest girls in the world, but now—seeing her in the dress they had given her—they had verifiable proof.

"Does it fit?" she asked them. "Do I look good?"

Both of them nodded, as they were still unable to speak.

A week later, Ronnie, Natalie's date for the prom, had the same reaction when he saw her walk down the same stairs in the same dress. He was so shocked by her beauty that he visibly shook when he helped her place the corsage he had bought around her wrist. He beamed with pride when they walked into the school gymnasium and every head turned to look at them. Even though Natalie was well-known and well liked by her peers, no one had ever considered that she was capable of looking so enchanting. It was thanks to the almost magical transforming powers of her red dress, that, in a dramatic upset, Natalie was voted prom queen that night instead of Joanne Hyams, who had been considered a shoo-in to take the crown.

Natalie wept with disbelief when her name was announced and everyone cheered and clapped. As they applauded her, she walked up the steps to the stage and joined the newly crowned prom king, Lance Bowrick, a popular member of the basketball team who just happened to be Joanne's boyfriend. There she accepted her plastic rhinestone tiara and walked back down the stairs to join her king in a dance. Ronnie was too excited about being the prom queen's date to become jealous that Natalie was dancing with a tall and handsome star athlete, but Joanne grew increasingly enraged as she watched her boyfriend dance with a girl who—as far as she was concerned—had stolen her crown.

What no one at the prom knew was that Joanne, who had come to the school in the 11th grade, had a history of violence. She had spent two years at a reform school after viciously attacking another girl in a shopping mall parking lot. After she had been released, her parents had decided to move to another town, partly so their daughter wouldn't face the stigma of being a young offender. In the year and a half that followed, Joanne had done a good job of controlling her rage, thanks mostly to the techniques she had learned from the reform school's counselors. But now, having lost a popularity contest she had been the absolute favorite to win and forced to watch her boyfriend dance with the tramp who had won it, she wasn't able to control her violent temper. To everyone's shocked surprise she started screaming at the top of her lungs and ran toward Natalie, who was unprepared to protect herself from Joanne's assault.

Joanne ripped Natalie out of Lance's arms and pummeled her with such force that the first blow knocked the innocent girl unconscious. This didn't stop Joanne, who kept pounding her victim until a group of boys dragged her away. She kicked and screamed and swore at them, and it took six of them to hold her down. As she struggled, a teacher called for the police and an ambulance.

The paramedics arrived first and rushed Natalie to the hospital. The police arrived a few minutes later and arrested Joanne for violent assault, but by the time they got to the police station they had to change the charge to second-degree murder. Joanne's blows to Natalie's head had caused the poor girl to develop an aneurysm, and she was dead before she made it to the emergency room.

Because of Joanne's violent record and the brutality of the assault, the district attorney attempted to have her tried as an adult, but her parents had hired a very good lawyer and he was able to persuade the judge to try her as a minor. He was also able to get the charge reduced to manslaughter, to which Joanne pled guilty. She was sentenced to go back to reform school until she turned 18, which was a year and two months away, and after that she would have to serve six years of probation, during which time she was ordered to seek psychiatric help.

Everyone who knew and loved Natalie was horrified by the light sentence her killer received, but they tried not to let this injustice turn them bitter. Instead they thought back to the great outpouring of love they had all felt at her funeral. As they were buoyed by their memories of Natalie's charm and constant good cheer, the sad event had felt less like a mourning of her death than a celebration of her life. Her parents had opted for an open casket, and they had decided to dress her in the beautiful red gown she had died in. Even though a case could be made that the dress had inadvertently led to her death, she had loved it so much and had looked so lovely wearing it that it was the obvious choice.

Many of the mourners felt compelled to deliver eulogies, so it had grown late by the time Natalie's father, who was to have the last word, got up to speak. He started by sharing some memories of his beloved daughter, but then surprised everyone by urging them to forgive Natalie's murderer for what she had done. He explained to them that Natalie would have been appalled to know that her death had left them with hate in their hearts, and that it would be a disservice to her memory to allow that anger to remain and build inside them.

Though his sentiments were genuine and did reflect the spirit of the daughter he had known, Natalie's father could not have been more wrong. Dying has a way of affecting a person's spirit, changing it for either good or ill, and the latter was true for his daughter. Upon being murdered, Natalie's spirit changed from that of a kind, forgiving young woman to that of a ruthless, avenging wraith. She did not want anyone to forgive Joanne. What she wanted was for her murderer to suffer. A lot.

Natalie's body was cremated and her ashes were kept in a small silver urn on the mantel above her parents' fireplace. It was there her spirit decided to make its home while it plotted ways to torment Joanne. It came up with hundreds of plans—each crueler than the last—but in the end there was only one obvious choice, and it was a killer.

Joanne had trouble sleeping at night at the reformatory. Her cot was uncomfortable, and the girl with whom she shared her small room suffered from night terrors that caused her to scream loudly in her sleep. Because it was against the rules to leave your bed or turn on a light after curfew, Joanne had no choice but to lie on her back and stare into the darkness. The building was always quiet, even during the day, but at night the silence could be terrifying. Joanne imagined, as she lay still on her bed and saw nothing but blackness and heard not a sound, that this was what it must feel like to be buried alive. The thought caused her to shiver and she tried to close her eyes and go back to sleep, but it was no use. The sensation of being buried overwhelmed her and kept her awake.

As she lay there trembling, her roommate began to scream. Joanne covered her ears with her hands, but she still heard the pathetic wails of the terrified girl beside her. She turned to her side, away from the girl and toward the wall. Even though the room had no windows and was pitch-black inside, Joanne gasped at what she saw when she faced the wall. It lasted for just a few seconds, but she was certain that she had seen it. It had glowed in the darkness, like a fluorescent mist. It had a face—one that she recognized. And though her hands had covered her ears, she was sure she had heard it speak to her.

"Your time will come," it had said. "You will suffer."

Over the next 14 months, this strange apparition visited Joanne at least 50 more times. Every time it did, it cursed her with threats of pain and misery, each one more specific than the last. The last night it appeared to her was the eve of her 18th birthday—the day she was due to be released back into society. Despite having grown used to the uncomfortable cot and the cries of her roommate, she could not sleep because of her excitement to be leaving the juvenile prison. She still, however, dreaded being awake at night, knowing that it might mean seeing the spirit that had tortured her so many times over the past year. Her fears proved justified when the misty wraith materialized above her.

"So you're going home, are you?" the spirit mocked her. "Well, you won't stay there for long. Not when you deserve to rot in the smallest, darkest cell the world has ever known. Enjoy your freedom! It will end before you know it."

With that the spirit faded away, leaving Joanne to shake uncontrollably in her bed, with tears streaming down her face. The two hours that it took for morning to arrive felt like days, and when the waking bell finally rang it sounded as glorious as any music she had ever heard. Quietly she got up, packed her belongings and said goodbye to her roommate. A counselor was waiting for her in the hallway and she followed him to the front office, where she was greeted with hugs from her parents. She was so happy and grateful to see them and touch them that when they asked her how she was doing, she said nothing about the spirit that had tortured her during all those sleepless nights.

"I'm good," she lied. "I'm ready to go home."

Even though she was exhausted, Joanne had trouble getting to sleep that first night in her old bed. It no longer felt like hers, and she tossed and turned as she tried to find a comfortable position. The longer she stayed awake, the more she began to fear that her phantom tormentor might reappear, but this time, mercifully, she was left alone.

Joanne had been released during the summer, and she and her parents had time to discuss what she should do about her education. She had been arrested before she had graduated and couldn't return to her old school for obvious reasons, so they decided to send her to Lucretia Academy, a private girls' school in the next town. They had to get permission from her probation officer, and—per the judge's orders—they had to find a psychiatrist for her to visit. With this done, Joanne left home once again and tried to get used to a new bed, this one located in a large room that held five other girls. The school's faculty was given all the details about her violent past, and suggested it would be best if the other students were not told.

For the next several months, Joanne's life was completely normal. Thanks to her natural charm and beauty, her peers, who never would have guessed that their new friend was capable of a horrible crime, quickly accepted her. Were it not for sporadic, but still terrifying, visits from the misty spirit, she would have had a very good time. She

never told anyone about the ghost who threatened her during the night, because—in her heart—she knew that she was being punished, and that her punishment was deserved. She wanted to admit this to her psychiatrist, her fear of being labeled as crazy held her back. To help with her depression, her doctor gave her a prescription for an antidepressant that had just come on the market.

With just one month of school left, Joanne learned that every year the girls at Lucretia Academy got together with the boys at the nearby Kloster Academy for a year-end dance. Joanne decided that this was her chance to have the prom experience she had missed out on. Excited by the prospect, she went out to find the perfect dress. The small town she was in didn't have much to offer in terms of fashionable clothing, but it did have the world's greatest used clothing store, so that was the first place she went.

At first it didn't look as if she was going to find anything, but then—almost by accident—she came upon a dress that almost made her faint when she saw it. It was a long, elegantly unadorned, bare-shouldered red dress, held up by thin, but sturdy, scarlet spaghetti straps. It was an exact replica of the dress Natalie had worn the night Joanne had beaten her to death. Even though she had to have recognized it, Joanne was more awed by the beauty of the gown than by the shock that came from this morbid coincidence. Imagining how glamorous she would look wearing it, she decided to buy it.

When she showed the dress to her roommates later that day, they all conceded that she was going to be the girl at the dance every boy would look at. They were right. When she walked into the Kloster Academy gymnasium, every male head turned to look at her. She wasn't there for two minutes before she received three different offers to dance. Though she would have loved to dance, she turned down the invitations. She wasn't feeling very well and was anxious because of another visit from the spirit the night before.

"This is the second to last time you're ever going to see me," the misty wraith had hissed at her. "For tomorrow is the day I finally get my revenge."

Terrified, Joanne had wanted to tell somebody about what she had been told, but—knowing that no one would believe her—all she could do was double the daily dose of her prescription, mistakenly believing that the extra pills would help calm her nerves.

As the music played, she stood beside the snack table and looked around for any sign of trouble. The longer she stood, the worse she felt. Her body felt numb, and it was getting harder and harder for her to breathe. Her skin began to sweat, and a knot of nausea tightened in her stomach. One of her roommates noticed that she didn't look well and walked over to her.

"Are you all right, Joanne?" she asked.

Before Joanne could answer, she felt her consciousness slip away and she collapsed to the floor. Her roommate called out for help and a teacher ran over to them. He tried to wake her, but when she would not stir he checked her pulse.

"She's…she's dead," he stammered.

An ambulance was called and the paramedics tried to revive her with no success. She was taken to the morgue, where an autopsy was scheduled to find out how she had died, but her parents stopped it. Their religious beliefs opposed any violation of a person's body after death, including autopsies, embalming and cremation. In keeping with their wishes, Joanne's body was buried the day after she died, her corpse still wearing the red dress.

As her body lay in its coffin 6 feet under the ground, a familiar mist materialized beside her right ear. It spoke to her.

"Wake up, Joanne," it whispered. "Wake up."

Slowly, Joanne's eyes opened. She saw nothing but complete darkness. The last thing she remembered was standing beside the snack table, watching others dance. She tried to move but found that wherever she was, she had no room to maneuver. She then pushed and hit everything around her, but it did no good. Within seconds she began to panic.

"Where am I?" she screamed.

"You're where I told you you'd end up," answered the spirit. "You're trapped in the world's smallest cell, and it is here where you are going to rot."

"I don't understand! How did this happen?"

"It happened because you're a very stupid girl who didn't know what would happen to you if you were exposed to formaldehyde while taking your medication. You didn't know that combining the two could cause a person's heartbeat and breath rate to slow down so much that the person would appear to be dead."

"But I never went anywhere near formaldehyde!"

"Your dressed is soaked in it!" laughed the spirit.

"But how?"

"Think about it!" chided the spirit. "Where had you seen that dress before?"

Joanne began to cry.

"It is just like the one Natalie wore that night," she admitted.

"No, it wasn't 'just like' it," the spirit corrected her. "It was *exactly* it."

"You don't mean…"

The spirit's voice changed. It became less empty and hollow and now sounded just like the girl it had belonged to in life.

"Yes, Joanne," Natalie's voice intoned, burning painfully into her victim's ears. "You're wearing my dress."

"No!" screamed Joanne. "That's not possible!"

"It is if the undertakers my parents hired were crooked enough to strip their dead clients naked before cremating them. It is if they then sold those dead people's clothes to the thrift store in the next town over. If that is the case, it is *very* possible. It is also very *just*. You killed me because of this dress, and now it's going to kill you."

Joanne began to scream wordlessly at the top of her lungs, but the soil absorbed her cries and drowned them out. She scratched at the coffin's lid with her nails until they broke off and blood began to seep down her fingers. By now too consumed by panic, she did not hear the last words Natalie's spirit spoke to her.

"Goodbye, Joanne," it whispered. "See you on the other side."

The Price of Doing Business

Jacob assumed he had misheard the large smiling man who sat in front of him.

"Excuse me," he said incredulously, "but did you just say that if I wanted to buy your company I would have to give you my right arm?"

The grin on Mr. Greenstreet's face stayed put as he wordlessly nodded, indicating that this multibillion-dollar business deal did in fact hinge on the youthful entrepreneur's willingness to sacrifice his most dominant limb.

"But that's insane!" Jacob protested.

Mr. Greenstreet shrugged. "It just may be," he admitted, "but that is my final term, and it is nonnegotiable. If you want to buy my company, you have to hand over your right arm, starting from the shoulder."

"But what could you possibly want with it?"

Mr. Greenstreet stood up from his desk and walked over to a door on the other side of the room. He opened it and indicated that Jacob was to follow him inside. Jacob got up and walked into the large room. Covered in gleaming white tile, the room was so bright he almost had to shade his eyes. But he quickly forgot the details of the room's design when he realized what it contained.

"This is my trophy room," explained Mr. Greenstreet. "This is what I have to show for my 50 years in the business."

Placed inside airtight showcases, on top of marble pedestals, were 27 severed limbs. Mostly arms, but several legs as well.

Mr. Greenstreet was obviously delighted by the look of horror on Jacob's face.

"You may think me a maniac," he smiled, "but, I assure you, every one of these trophies was given to me willingly, and no one regrets making the sacrifice."

Jacob felt nauseated. "I think I'm going to be sick," he said as the full reality of his situation became apparent.

The problem was that, even though his every impulse demanded that he run out of the room and get as far away from this madman as he could, he needed to make this deal happen too much to back away. A millionaire since he was 17, when he had developed a computer program that revolutionized the industry, Jacob had spent the last 10 years building an empire that was almost unrivaled in the world of big business. But he alone knew that the backbone of his company—the program that had started it all a decade earlier—was, despite years and years of new versions and upgrades, still fatally flawed. So far he had been able to keep the program's potentially disastrous bug from being discovered, but he knew it was only a matter of time, and once it was found out his company would become worthless. But all was not hopeless. Thanks to the efforts of the spies he employed at his competitors, he had discovered that Greenstreet's company had developed a new program that could—by a fluke of code—permanently fix the bug and ensure the survival of his corporation. He needed that program, and buying Greenstreet's company was the only way he could get it.

"As sickened as you may feel," Mr. Greenstreet noted, "you cannot have totally dismissed the thought, or else you would have run out of here by now."

Jacob bent over to catch his breath as the blood drained from his head. He felt faint, and it took him several minutes before he had the strength to stand up straight and speak.

"How would you want it done?" he asked.

Mr. Greenstreet's grin grew even wider as he began to explain the process by which Jacob's arm would be removed.

"I am afraid I am very particular about how it must be done. For example, I must insist that you be awake when the arm is amputated and that anesthetic will be administered only afterwards."

Jacob gritted his teeth at the thought of this. "And how is it supposed to be removed?" he asked, not really wanting to know.

Mr. Greenstreet walked over to a closed cabinet in the corner of the room. He took out a key from a pocket inside his suit jacket and used it to open the heavy oak door. Jacob's eyes widened in disbelief as the large man took out what looked like an ornate samurai sword.

Noting the look in Jacob's eyes, Mr. Greenstreet attempted to reassure him.

"You will not find a blade sharper than this anywhere," he insisted. "All it will take is one fast blow for me to remove the entire arm. An ambulance with paramedics is waiting downstairs, and they will rush you to a private hospital within minutes. It will all be over so quickly, it will seem less troublesome than a visit to the dentist."

"Why don't I believe that?" asked Jacob.

"Whether you believe it or not, I can tell by the look in your eyes that you've already decided to go through with it."

Jacob no longer felt sick. Now all he felt was cold and numb.

"Let's get it over with," he muttered resignedly.

Mr. Greenstreet put the sword back into the cabinet and headed back to his office. "We have some paperwork to sign before we can begin," he explained.

Jacob followed him back into the office and signed a short contract, which indicated that he willingly sacrificed his arm to Humphrey Greenstreet and would not attempt in any way to get it back or seek legal action against its new owner. Five minutes later he found himself in a different room. This one was definitely not gleaming white, as its walls and floor were stained with what Jacob could only assume was blood. Mr. Greenstreet placed Jacob's right hand into a heavy metal cuff attached to a metal chain that hung from the roof. Jacob's arm stretched straight out, and he closed his eyes while the older man stood behind him with the razor-sharp sword. Mr. Greenstreet raised the sword into the air and started to count down from three. When he got to one, he brought the sword down with as much power as he could.

🕷 🕷 🕷

Jacob woke in a hospital room. With his mind clouded by painkillers, his vision was hazy and he could barely make out what the voice speaking to him was saying. He looked to his side and saw what looked like the face of a beautiful woman in her early 40s. He had never seen her before, but she spoke to him by name.

"Do you know who I am, Mr. Fence?" she asked him.

He shook his head.

"My name is Camilla Greenstreet. Humphrey Greenstreet is my husband."

"Nice to meet ya," Jacob slurred his words. His brain made the attempt to offer his right hand to shake with hers, but it was stymied by his lack of an arm.

"I wish I could tell you that my visit is purely a social one," she said to him, "but I am afraid that my purpose here is business related."

"What's the matter," Jacob muttered, "doesn't he like the arm?"

"I'm sure he loves it," said Camilla, "but the problem is, it wasn't his to ask for."

"I don't understand."

"I hate to tell you this," she said sincerely, "but my husband had no right to sell you the company. He does not own it. I do."

As dazed as he had been, this shock was enough to waken Jacob from his drug-induced stupor. Camilla's revelation hit him like an ice-water tidal wave. His senses restored, he looked at her and gasped at what he saw. The beauty of her face had kept him from noticing that she sat immobile in a wheelchair, dressed in a stylish suit that must have been hand-tailored for her since it had no arms or legs.

"And as you can see, in order to own the company, I had to sacrifice a lot to get it," she admitted with a knowing smile.

Theodore

Bobby laughed with delight as he opened his last Christmas present. Tearing away the wrapping paper, he saw a furry face stare out at him from behind a plastic window, and he knew exactly who it was. It was Theodore the Talking Bear. Every day for the past six months he had told his parents—and everyone else he knew—that Santa's elves were building him a Theodore, and he had been right all along.

"I told ya!" he shouted at his older brother, Eric, who had expressed his doubts about Bobby's much-repeated assertion. "They built me the one I wanted!"

"Yeah, whatever," Eric sighed, much too blasé at 11 to get excited by anything as lame as Christmas presents.

Bobby didn't even bother to take off all the present's wrapping before he opened up the box and pulled out his new toy. Theodore was covered head to toe in fluffy brown fur, and his face was dominated by a huge happy grin. Bobby found the power switch and flicked it on, but nothing happened.

Eric rolled his eyes. "You have to put the batteries in, doofus."

"Dad!" Bobby shouted over to his father, who was admiring the bottle of aftershave lotion that Eric had bought him. "Theodore needs batteries!"

Ten minutes later, batteries had been found and Theodore was all ready to go. Bobby flicked on the power switch and this time his new toy buzzed to life.

"Hello," the bear greeted Bobby, with a voice that sounded both good-natured and slightly silly. "My name is Theodore Lionel Worthington Bear the Third, but you can call me Theodore. What's your name?"

"I'm Bobby."

"Well…" the toy said, and paused for a microsecond, "Bobby…it's a pleasure to meet you!"

Bobby couldn't believe what he had just heard.

"Whoa! He just said my name!" he told his brother.

"So what?" sneered Eric. "It just means he's got a microchip inside him. It's not like he's *alive* or anything."

Despite his brother's derision, Bobby fell in love with his new toy. He was old and smart enough to know Eric was right in saying that Theodore wasn't really alive, but sometimes it sure did seem that he was. He was often amazed by the things Theodore could say and do, and one morning he decided to show off the toy's unique skills to his classmates.

"This is Theodore," he told them during show-and-tell. "He's a bear and he's *really* smart. Let me show you." With that he turned Theodore on.

"Hello, my name is Theodore Lionel Worthington Bear the Third, but you can call me Theodore," the toy introduced itself.

Bobby's classmates were not impressed.

"I've got plenty of toys that talk," one bored little girl informed Bobby.

"But he talks back!" Bobby explained to them. "Just listen." He turned to his toy and spoke to it. "How are you doing today, Theodore?"

Several long and painful moments of silence followed before Theodore answered him.

"Hello, my name is Theodore Lionel Worthington Bear the Third, but you can call me Theodore."

Bobby's classmates frowned at him.

"He just said that!" complained one boy.

"That's the stupidest toy ever!" hooted another.

"C'mon, Theodore," Bobby pleaded. "Say something."

"Would you like to hear me sing a song?" asked Theodore, and before Bobby could respond, the toy started to sing—something it had never done before. "I'm Theodore, Theodore, the big brown bear that you adore. Theodore, Theodore, the furry friend you can't ignore. Theodore, Theodore, the fabulous talking bear!"

Now the kids started to boo, and Bobby's teacher made him put Theodore away and sit down. He couldn't understand what had just happened. Theodore had never acted like that before, like a...a...stupid *toy*. When he got home from school, he was so mad at Theodore that he didn't even bother to take him out of his knapsack. And then, when bedtime came, Bobby was so tired he forgot all about Theodore, and for the first time since Christmas, he went to sleep without his favorite toy at his side.

Bobby wasn't a good sleeper. He was an imaginative little boy and suffered from lots of nightmares because of his always-active mind. Thanks to these bad dreams he often woke up in the middle of the night, and tonight offered no exception. He had dreamed that a great big scaly monster, with sharp claws and long, jagged teeth, was chasing after him. The faster Bobby ran, the more tired he became, and he began to fall and trip on his own leaden feet. He woke up just as the monster caught him and smiled wickedly, preparing to take its first bite.

Bobby could feel his heart pound under the covers as his eyes burst open. They were still blurry from sleep and all he could make out was the faint glow of his night-light. For a second he considered getting out of bed and telling his parents about his dream, but he decided not to, because they always seemed annoyed when he woke them. Instead, he reached over to grab Theodore for a hug, but the bear wasn't there. It was then that Bobby remembered he had left his favorite toy in his knapsack, and he decided to go get it. He rubbed the sleep out of his eyes and then, as quietly as he could, he slowly got out of bed and tiptoed out of his room. He made his way to the kitchen and, with the help of the moonlight shining through the window, he spotted his bag. He walked over to it, opened it and was surprised to find that Theodore wasn't there. Confused, he tiptoed back to his room and climbed back into bed. As he lay there he tried to think of what could have happened to his toy, until, finally, a big yawn came over him and he stretched out his arms. To his shock and surprise he felt the familiar sensation of soft fur against his skin. He turned his head and saw Theodore, lying down in his regular spot.

"Ahhhhhhhhhhh!" Bobby screamed with fright as he jumped out of bed and ran to his parents. "Mom! Dad!" he shouted loudly as he tried to wake them up.

"Bobby, stop that," his mother ordered him angrily, her voice heavy with sleep. "Be quiet and go back to bed. Your father has to get up early tomorrow."

"But Theodore—" he tried to explain to her.

"Now is not the time to tell us what your toy can do," she insisted. "Go back to bed or you'll be too tired to get any work done at school tomorrow."

"But—" Bobby tried to protest.

"Now!"

Bobby hung his head and walked out of his parents' bedroom. He lingered for several minutes in the hallway before he worked up the courage to go back into his room. As he walked in, the hair on his neck stood up when he saw that Theodore was no longer lying at the side of his bed but was instead sitting upright in the middle of it.

"Hello, Bobby," the furry toy greeted the young boy.

"H-h-how did you do that?" Bobby asked him, his voice breaking with fear.

"I can do a lot of things," Theodore replied cheerfully. "I'm a wonderful toy!"

"If you're so wonderful, then why didn't you do anything cool yesterday at show-and-tell?"

"Because I can only do these wonderful things for you."

"Why?"

"Because you believe in me," explained Theodore. "No one else has the kind of faith that you do."

"Really?"

"It's the truth, Bobby," said Theodore solemnly. "You're a very special boy. Now come back to bed. If you don't, you'll be tired at school tomorrow."

Feeling reassured, Bobby climbed back into bed and hugged Theodore close to him as he fell back to sleep. For the first time, Theodore hugged Bobby back.

In the months that followed, Bobby spent all his free time at home playing with his seemingly magical toy. Theodore could do practically anything when the two of them were alone. He could run and jump and dance; he could play card games like Go Fish and Crazy Eights; he could even play video games, though he was admittedly pretty easy to beat, since he didn't have any thumbs to work with. But as soon as someone else walked into the room, Theodore would suddenly become inert and fall to the floor. All the life would drain out of him, and he would be capable of uttering only 20 or so prerecorded sentences.

At first these abrupt changes in Theodore's behavior had struck Bobby as incredibly strange, but the more they happened, the less he thought to question them. Sometimes, though, he swore he could see a glint of life in Theodore's eyes even when another person's presence had supposedly caused him to turn back into a normal toy. It was as if the magical little bear was only *pretending* to be a toy, but Bobby could think of no good reason for this to be true. It wasn't until something happened with his older brother that he began to question everything Theodore had told him.

It had been a quiet Saturday afternoon, and Eric was bored. Like many older brothers, he figured that a good way to combat his boredom would be to torture his little brother, so he barged into Bobby's room and started bugging him by talking about a girl Bobby had a crush on.

"Whatcha doin', brat? Dreaming about Molly Mitchell?"

As always, Theodore had flopped to the floor as soon as Eric walked into the room.

"Leave me alone," Bobby protested. "I didn't do anything to you."

"Don't be such a whiner, brat," Eric sneered. "Molly Mitchell won't like you if you're a big wussy whiner."

"I'm not a whiner and I don't like Molly Mitchell!" Bobby shouted passionately at Eric, even though he was lying about the last part.

"You *are* a whiner and you *la-hove* Molly Mitchell," Eric teased.

"Shut up!"

"Make me, brat!"

Bobby ran toward his brother, who pushed him down easily with a hard shove.

"You're going to have to do better than that, brat," he laughed.

Bobby tried not to cry as he got up, but he couldn't help it.

"Sheesh," Eric said, rolling his eyes. "A whiner *and* a crybaby. Molly Mitchell is—ahhhhhhhhhhhhhhhhhhhh!" Eric screamed out with pain. Bobby watched, stunned, as his brother turned around, and he saw that Theodore was biting down hard on Eric's butt. Eric turned his head to see what was biting him, but he couldn't see Theodore behind him. "Get it off! Get it off!" he screamed at Bobby, who did as he was told, but not in a big hurry. As soon as he touched Theodore, the bear flopped into his hands, as if he had been lifeless all along. Eric ran crying out of Bobby's room, holding his sore bottom in his hands. When he was gone, Theodore came back to life.

"That'll teach him," he said to Bobby.

"What did you do that for?" asked Bobby.

"I didn't like the way he was picking on you."

"But I thought you couldn't do stuff like that when other people were around."

Theodore paused for a second, as if he had been caught at something.

"Yeah, that's true, but your brother…had his back to me, so he couldn't see me," he explained uncomfortably, "and since he couldn't see me, I could move while he was in the room. That makes sense, doesn't it?"

"I guess," Bobby said, sounding unconvinced.

After that he kept a very close eye on his toy. One day it occurred to him that Theodore's batteries hadn't been changed since that first Christmas morning, which meant they had to have died by now. When he asked Theodore about this, the bear explained that as long as Bobby believed in him, he didn't need batteries. This sounded reasonable to Bobby, so he didn't bring it up again. After that, despite his close watch, nothing strange happened for a long time.

But then one day Bobby's father decided to clean up the basement, and he asked Bobby to help him. Bobby left Theodore in his room and went to work, throwing junk into plastic garbage bags that were going to the dump. While he was going through the various items strewn around the basement, he found something that gave him goose bumps. Behind a cardboard box full of old toys, he found a strange robotic skeleton that was covered with soft foam. It looked as if somebody had taken the skin off a complicated toy. Bobby looked into the toy's hard plastic eyes and recognized them. He found the toy's power switch and turned it on to see if it still worked.

"Hello," the toy said, "my name is Theodore Lionel Worthington Bear the Third, but you can call me Theodore. What's your name?"

Bobby screamed.

"Well…" The toy paused for a microsecond before it replicated his scream. "Ahhhhhhhhhhhhhh…it's a pleasure to meet you!"

Bobby dropped the toy and ran up to his room.

"What are you?" he asked Theodore breathlessly when he got there.

"What do you mean?" Theodore answered innocently. "I'm a toy."

"No, you're not! I found the insides of the real Theodore in the basement!"

"You what?" Theodore's voice changed suddenly, becoming deeper and more frightening.

"I found it," Bobby repeated.

"You listen to me, kid," the bear growled. "You'd better forget what you found down there. It's for your own good."

"I don't believe you!"

"You'd better believe me, kid! 'Cause you'll regret it if—"

Before Theodore could finish what he was saying, Bobby ran up to him and grabbed him. The toy struggled in his arms and tried to bite him, but Bobby managed to hold on to him. As quickly as he could, he tore off bits of Theodore's fur with one hand.

"Stop it!" Theodore screamed, but Bobby didn't listen. As he tore away the fur that covered Theodore's body, he saw that underneath it was a kind of dry, reptilian skin. Finally, Theodore was able to sink his teeth into one of Bobby's fingers, and the pain caused him to drop the toy.

When Theodore hit the floor, his stitches—weakened by the damage Bobby had inflicted—burst open and revealed a small gremlin-like creature with green scaly skin and sharp jagged teeth.

"Now you done it, kid," the greenish imp said, shaking its head. "My kind can be the best friends a little boy could ever have, but we have a rule. It's as simple as it is unbreakable. The boys can never know what we really look like, and if they find out, then there is only one thing we can do. WE HAVE TO EAT THEM!"

Bobby froze with fright as the small creature began to suddenly grow in front of him. Within seconds it was as big as he was, and within a few more it towered over him. No matter how much Bobby's brain warned him to run, his feet wouldn't listen. Now much more of a monster than a strange creature, it lunged at him with its claws extended. Bobby screamed as it picked him up and opened its mouth. It was the loudest scream anyone had ever screamed in the history of the world.

With a start, Bobby woke from his dream. His room was dark, save for the glow of his night-light. His heart raced as he slowly realized that he had just had another one of his nightmares. This one had seemed more realistic than any other he'd experienced, and it took him a few minutes before he calmed down enough to go back to sleep. When he finally felt relaxed enough to close his eyes, he grabbed hold of Theodore, who had been lying on his usual spot on Bobby's bed, and gave him a hug.

He was far too tired to notice that Theodore hugged him back.

It Can't Find You in the Dark

Neil felt tired as he slipped into his jacket and picked up his briefcase. Talking to Mrs. Davis about the death of her husband, Laurence, always took something out of him. The way she went on and on about having to take care of him after the stroke and the loneliness that she felt now that he was gone made Neil just want to grab her and shake her and scream, "He's dead! Get over it already!" But he never did. He had learned over the years that the greatest skill a psychiatrist needed to hone was not the talent to listen compassionately or effectively diagnose a person's neurosis, but the ability to keep from accusing patients of being big fat stupid whiners.

Ready to go, he walked out of his office and said goodbye to Dyanna, his secretary, who was finishing up in his waiting room. Before she had a chance to return his farewell, the door to the waiting room burst open. The man who came in ran over to Neil and fell to his knees, sobbing like a terrified child.

"Dr. Procter," he wept, "you've got to help me. I can't get rid of it. It follows me wherever I go!"

Neil looked down and recognized the man as a former patient named Wilson Styck. A gambling addict, he had been forced by the courts to see Neil after he had been convicted of embezzling from the company he worked for to pay off the debt he owed a particularly notorious bookmaker. Wilson had never taken his therapy seriously and stopped seeing Neil as soon as the judge let him.

"Calm down," Neil urged the panic-stricken man. "If you talk to Dyanna here, you can set up an appointment—"

"This can't wait!" Wilson interrupted. "I have to see you now! It's only a matter of time!"

"Until what?" asked Neil.

"Until it gets me!"

"Until what gets you?"

Wilson shook his head. "I can't tell you in here. It's right behind me. It can see and hear everything I say to you."

"Fine," said Neil, trying to hide his displeasure. "Can it see and hear you in my office?"

"No," answered Wilson, "that's why I came to you!"

"All right then. Step into my office and we'll talk about what's bothering you."

Wilson got off his knees and ran into the empty office. Neil sighed and told Dyanna to call his wife to tell her that he was going to be late before he followed the obviously deranged man into the room.

When he walked in, he found Wilson sitting in a chair in the dark. Neil went over to turn on a light, but Wilson stopped him.

"Keep it off!" he shouted. "It needs the light to follow me. I was trying to think of places to go and people I could talk to and I remembered that your office had no windows, so the sun couldn't get into it."

"What's going on?" asked Neil.

"I can't get rid of it. It follows me everywhere. Sometimes it's behind me, sometimes it's in front of me, sometimes it's beside me, but the only time it's not there at all is when I'm in the dark."

"What are you talking about?"

"You won't understand. I have to start at the beginning. I have to tell you why it won't leave me alone."

Neil sat down at his desk, but not before he bumped his shin in the dark.

"Then tell me," he said as he sat back in his chair.

After his conviction, Wilson had gone two years without making a single bet, but his abstention ended as soon as he was no longer forced to see Dr. Procter or report to his probation officer. Literally 10 minutes after his court-appointed obligations ended for good, he called Keeler, his old bookie, and bet on a football game. Within a week he was down $25,000, having made a series of enormous bets to make up for what he felt he should have won during his two years of gambling abstinence. Within a month that figured quadrupled. Getting desperate, he heard about a sure thing and bet everything he owed. His debt doubled when the sure thing proved not to be so certain.

After a long drunken night in a cheap motel room, he discovered that he did not have the heart to kill himself, so he did the only thing he could do—he pleaded to those he owed money to to let him do anything to pay his debt off. Keeler, the first person Wilson had called when he started gambling again, was also the first person to take advantage of this plea.

Wilson found himself sitting on a plastic lawn chair in Keeler's dank office, a small room at the back of a run-down bowling alley. Wilson was nervous. His stomach churned and his ulcer responded by making him grit his teeth with pain. Keeler was casually chewing on a messy sandwich from the deli across the street while he sat behind a small desk that had been stolen from an office supply warehouse.

"You tell me you'll do anything, huh?" Keeler sighed. "How much do you owe me?" He looked up and addressed a lackey who was standing by the door. "How much does this monkey owe me?"

"Fifty-three grand," answered the man Wilson had never seen before.

"You're going to have to do a lot of anything to pay off $53,000. Most people have to work two years doing anything to make that kind of money."

"Seriously, Keeler," Wilson pleaded. "I'll do whatever you want!"

"There is nothing I want that costs $53,000, but I suppose you can do a bunch of little things and lower that number a little."

"Whatever you want," Wilson agreed, "I'm your man."

Keeler nodded his head toward the lackey, and the large man reached into his jacket and pulled out a small revolver. He handed it to Wilson, who had never held a gun before in his life.

"What do you want me to do with this?" he asked, confused.

"I want you to eat it," Keeler said sarcastically. "What do you think I want you to do with it?"

"I couldn't shoot somebody," said Wilson.

"Look, you said you'd do anything, and this is what you have to do. If you want, I can have Freddie take the gun back and break both of your arms and legs to remind you that you are not in a position to be choosy."

Wilson stared at the gun in his hands. He felt as if he was going to throw up.

"If I do it," he asked, his voice barely above a whisper, "how much will you let me off for?"

Keeler finished his sandwich and sat back in his chair, which had also been stolen from an office supply company.

"You gotta understand," he explained. "The business isn't like it used to be. Ten years ago it used to be tough to find someone willing to kill for money, but these days," he shrugged, "you got guys lining up to do it for almost nothing. A pro these days is lucky if he can get ten grand to do a job. You ain't that lucky and you ain't a pro. Pull this off and I'll forget five grand of what you owe. And if you don't mess it up too badly, I may let you do it again."

Wilson stayed quiet for a very long time as he stared at the gun and asked himself if it was worth taking another person's life just so he didn't owe this ugly thug $5000.

"Who do I have to kill?" he asked when he finally decided that it was.

"A deadbeat. Just like you. Owes me 97 grand. He tried to pay it off the same way you're going to, but he made a mess of his first job and got the cops after him. They can't find him, but I know where he is. Freddie's going to take you there and you're going to get rid of him for me."

"What's his name?" asked Wilson

"What do you care?" sneered Keeler. "Just shut up and do it."

Two hours later Wilson found himself in a beat-up truck parked outside a shack in the woods. Freddie was behind the wheel and he looked impatiently at his terrified passenger.

"Whaddaya waitin' for?" asked the large man. "He ain't gonna die by you just sittin' there."

Wilson closed his eyes and grabbed the revolver from his jacket pocket and stepped out of the truck. He had felt sick since he had left Keeler's office. He walked slowly to the shack's door, took a deep breath and tried to open it. The door had no lock and it swung open. It was pitch-black inside. Cardboard and tinfoil had been taped over the windows to stop any light from getting in.

"Close the door!" shouted a voice from the left-hand back corner of the shack. "You're letting in the light! The only place it can't follow you is in the dark!"

"Keeler sent me," Wilson explained.

"So you're here to kill me?" asked the voice.

"Yes," answered Wilson.

"Thank God!" the man shouted as he jumped up and ran past Wilson out the door into the daylight. "Quick! Do it now! Let it see! It won't be able to follow me when I'm dead!"

"Are you crazy?" asked Wilson.

"Yes! If that makes you pull the trigger, then yes! Put me out of my misery! Do it! Now!"

Wilson's stomach churned as he raised the weapon. He closed his eyes and pulled the trigger six times until the gun was out of bullets. When he opened them again he saw the man lying dead on the ground. Wilson dropped the gun and bent over and threw up.

Freddie got out of the truck and walked over to him.

"You did good, man," he complimented Wilson. "And don't worry. I threw up my first time too. It gets easier," he admitted with a shrug.

"Guy was crazy," panted Wilson, "he *wanted* me to kill him."

"Nothin' wrong with that," said Freddie. "He could have wanted to live and made your job a whole lot tougher."

Wilson threw up again, and he stood there with Freddie for several minutes before he felt well enough to get back in the truck. It was getting late in the day, but it was the middle of summer and the sun was still high in the sky. Wilson squinted as they drove away from the shack. The light hurt his eyes. Freddie turned on the radio and fiddled with the stations until he found the baseball game. Wilson tried not to listen to it, as he hadn't had a chance to bet on the game and the team he would have chosen to win was ahead by 10 runs. More proof that he could only pick a winner when it didn't count.

An hour passed and the sun still shone brightly. As time passed Wilson felt his neck grow warm and his little hairs began to rise up. Though he had no explanation for it, he felt as though he was being watched. He turned around and looked out the truck's back window and saw only the quiet road. His skin tingled and he scratched at it. Out of the corner of his eye he thought he saw something and turned toward the back window again as fast as he could. There was still nothing there.

"What's the matter with you?" asked Freddie.

"Nothing," he lied. "Still feeling a little sick is all."

"If you're going to puke again, roll down the window."

"I'll be okay," insisted Wilson, even though he wasn't sure he was right.

They got back to the city and Freddie dropped Wilson off at the cheap motel he was living in. As soon as he stepped out of the truck, he became certain that he was being watched. As Freddie drove away, Wilson spun around on the motel's parking lot to catch sight of the person spying on him. He couldn't find him, but he knew he was there. He ran to his motel and locked himself inside. He closed the drapes over the window, but that didn't ease his paranoia.

"They've got cameras in here," he muttered to himself.

He turned off all the lights, but, knowing that cameras could use infrared vision to see in the dark, he hid under the bed to make sure no one saw him.

When the morning came, the sun was so bright even his closed curtains couldn't keep it away. He struggled from under the bed and decided he had to have something to eat. He walked cautiously out of his motel room toward the fast food restaurant down the block. With each step he felt the presence of whoever was stalking him. No matter how fast he walked, the person was always right behind him. He kept turning around quickly, in the hope of catching him, but the person was always too quick for him.

He ate quickly and ran back to his motel room. He wasn't there 10 minutes when his phone rang. He was so nervous he answered it on instinct, not even thinking that the caller might be the person following him. It wasn't. It was Keeler.

"So I hear you did a good job yesterday," he told Wilson.

"Uh-huh," Wilson muttered.

"Wanna do it again? Get another five Gs off your vig."

"Yeah, sure, whatever," said Wilson, not even sure what he was agreeing to.

"Good. Come over to the bowling alley in half an hour."

"Yeah, okay."

Wilson didn't go to the bowling alley. Instead he found a room at a different motel, hoping to escape from his stalker. It didn't work. Whoever was following him was so good he had already managed to sneak into the room and hide. Wilson tore the room apart searching for him, with no luck. He sat in the dark for several hours before he realized why his pursuer had thus far proven so hard to catch. It was not a man who was following him, but a man's ghost, and there was only one person in the world with reason enough to haunt him.

"You said you wanted me to kill you!" he pleaded to it. "You told me to shoot you! Leave me alone! Please!"

He moved to another motel, but the spirit followed him again. It seemed as though it was attached to him. It only went away in the dark, but even then he could tell it was close by.

At first it seemed intent on merely following him, but as the days passed it became clearer to Wilson that it intended to do more than keep him company.

"What are you going to do?" he asked it, but it refused to tell him.

One morning he woke up when he heard knocking on his motel room door. He didn't answer it and the door burst open. It was Freddie. He had a gun in his hand.

"Keeler's been lookin' for you, buddy. Thought you disappeared from him, huh? It don't work like that. You don't disappear when you owe the kinda money you owe."

He raised the gun at Wilson, who felt his mind go completely blank. For a minute his brain registered absolutely nothing. Then he heard a loud shot. This brought him back and he looked and saw that Freddie's gun was in his hand. A broken lamp lay beside Freddie on the ground, and it looked as if it had been used to bash in the man's head. He smelled the smoke from the gun's muzzle and saw that he had just shot another man dead.

He turned away from the body and looked at the wall. All he saw was his shadow. It was bigger than it had been before, as if something had suddenly caused it to double in size.

"That's where you've been!" he shouted at it. "You've been hiding in my shadow! And now you have someone else with you!"

He turned and ran out of the motel room, but his shadow followed him wherever he went. And with each step he became more certain that it was plotting against him, that it would take revenge against him for his crimes and that the revenge would be far worse than anything he had ever done.

As he ran he tried to think of some place he could go, maybe some place where he could get some help, some place dark.

🕷 🕷 🕷

"That's why I'm here, Doc," Wilson explained to Neil. "Tell me what does a guy do when his shadow has it in for him?"

Neil didn't say anything.

"C'mon!" Wilson shouted. "You got to have an answer for me!"

Neil tried his best.

"It's just guilt. That's all. You've done horrible things and they are weighing heavily upon your conscience. Your shadow isn't after you. You're after yourself. Your paranoia is nothing more than a psychotic reaction to a traumatic event."

"No!" Wilson screamed. "It's real! You don't know! It's real! Real!"

"Wilson, it's obvious that you don't want to be helped. I want you to leave."

"Please Doc!" Wilson pleaded. "You're my last hope."

"No, I'm not," Neil disagreed. "I can't help you. Now if you don't leave I will be forced to call the police."

Wilson became quiet and slowly got out of his chair.

"You're doing me in, Doc," he said before he left. "You're doing me in."

Neil sighed with relief when Wilson was finally gone.

"What was that all about?" asked Dyanna as she poked her head in through his door. "And why is it so dark in here?"

"You just saw a very sick man," Neil explained. "I almost feel sorry for him."

Dyanna started to say something, but she was interrupted by the sounds of screams and a loud horrible crash. They both ran into the hallway to investigate. There they saw a stunned janitor shaking in front of the elevator.

"What happened?" asked Neil.

"I don't believe it," the janitor whispered.

"What happened?" asked Dyanna.

"There was a man waiting for the elevator. He looked all sweaty and nervous and kept looking over his shoulder at his shadow. The elevator's doors opened and he was about to step in, when he saw that the elevator wasn't there, just the empty shaft. He stopped himself and then…"

"What?" asked Neil.

"You won't believe me," the janitor insisted, "but I swear that what I saw happen next was that the man's shadow"—he shook his head disbelievingly—"it rose off the floor. Like it was alive! And it pushed him! I swear to God it pushed him!"

Neil's heart froze in his chest.

"But what was that crash?" asked Dyanna.

"That's the thing," said the janitor. "It don't mean anything to be pushed down the shaft right here. We're only on the second floor. I looked down to see if the man was okay and he was just fine, but then from above me I heard the elevator's cables make a funny noise. I lifted my head out, and two seconds later the cables snapped and the elevator fell all the way down. The guy didn't have a chance."

As the three of them stood there in shocked silence, they heard sirens blare from outside building.

The janitor took off his glasses and wiped tears and sweat from out of his eyes. He turned toward Neil and spoke with a very shaky voice.

"You're a shrink, right?" he asked. "Can you tell me? Was what I saw the craziest thing you've ever heard?"

Give Me a Head with Hair

When Winslow Mortimer was a teenager, he would have loved to be cursed with acne. If the worst thing he had to deal with growing up was a few pimples and blackheads, he would have considered himself blessed. Instead, while the other kids scrubbed their skin with alcohol pads and applied the latest zit remedy, Winslow was forced to watch defenselessly as the long brown mane of hair he had nurtured since grade eight started to fall out in clumps.

He was just 16 when he started to go bald. The doctors said he had alopecia universalis, which meant that inside his body a multitude of confused white blood cells were waging a cruel war against his unarmed hair follicles. He was destined to lose not just all the hair on his head, but all the hair on his body as well. It seemed particularly cruel that just as he started to grow hair on his chest, it started to fall out.

Some men can pull off the cue ball look quite well. Winslow wasn't one of them. He had an odd-shaped head, which, helped by his pale skin, looked exactly like a freshly laid egg. His peers were not kind and took every opportunity to make fun of his unfortunate condition. The list of names they called him was so long a person could spend a good half a day reciting it.

As he grew older, Winslow started to wear wigs and glue-on fake eyebrows, but he could never afford to buy anything that didn't look ridiculous. If people weren't making fun of his funny-shaped bald head, they were laughing at how stupid he looked in the obvious toupee.

His condition made hair transplant surgery impossible, and he couldn't have afforded it in any case. Years of other people's cruel mockery eventually turned him into a very bitter person. He didn't have any friends, and he found it difficult to hold on to a job for longer than a few months.

The worse his life became, the more he believed that he would have been happy and successful if he had only been able to keep his long brown mane. He could have been a rock star or a male model or even just a successful salesman. He tried to fight his depression using booze, and every time he got drunk he would spend the night looking at himself in the mirror with one of his horrible wigs on, crying and wishing someone would invent a time machine so he could go back and remember what it was like when he had hair.

One morning, after a particularly long bout of sobbing in front of the mirror the night before, Winslow woke up with a hangover so horrible he felt as if his head was the clapper in one of the bells of Notre Dame. Groggy and nauseated, he blearily made his way to his small kitchenette and made himself a mug of instant coffee. As he finished stirring it, he walked over and collapsed on the couch. Slowly he sipped at the coffee and noticed that yesterday's newspaper was still lying unread on the collection of plywood and cinder blocks he used as a table. He opened the paper to the classified section to see whether any new jobs were posted, but as always there was nothing besides the usual requests for door-to-door salesmen and telemarketers. He was about to throw the paper away when another ad caught his eye.

Do you suffer from alopecia universalis? If you do, then rejoice—a cure has been found! Contact Mme. Fortinbras at 555-9873 to find out more.

Winslow looked at the ad wearily. Con artists willing to exploit his desire for hair had scammed him before. But then he took a good look around at his apartment and felt the agonizing throb of his head and decided that it was worth the risk. Right then and there he picked up the phone and gave Mme. Fortinbras a call.

Later that day he found himself knocking on a rotting wooden door to a decrepit old apartment on the bad side of town. Considering the surroundings and the way the woman had sounded on the phone, Winslow was shocked by how young she turned out to be when she opened the door. She had to be at least 10 years younger than he was, just barely out of her teens. Her features were both softly feminine and attractively well defined. Her voice was the same as it had been over the phone, huskily European.

"Winslow?" she asked upon seeing him.

Always nervous around attractive women, he nodded quietly. She let him in.

"Before you go one step farther, I demand that you remove that hideous thing at once," she ordered him as soon as he stepped inside.

Meekly, he obeyed, removing the awful wig he had worn on the way over to her apartment.

"I'll have those as well," she insisted, holding out her open palm to collect the glue-on eyebrows he had been wearing.

He peeled them off his brow and handed them to her.

"Now we can do business," she smiled at him. "Come, come," she urged, motioning for him to follow. Her small apartment was separated into several rooms by enormous stacks of old books that served as makeshift walls. She pulled him along until they were in a space with a small folding card table and two cheap plastic lawn chairs. She urged him to sit down, which he did immediately. It had been so long since he had had the attention of an attractive young woman, she could have asked him to stand on his head and bark like a dog and he would have happily complied.

She sat down in the other chair and started into what he assumed was her sales spiel.

"It is not easy having no hair. Many do not know this, but it is true. We women spend countless hours of our days removing the hair from our bodies, cursing the effort it takes. Would we complain so much if we were so horribly cursed as you? If we had no hair to remove at all? I do not think so!"

Winslow had the sense that she had just made some kind of point, so he nodded his head in agreement.

"But there is no curse that the magicks cannot cure. The question is, are you willing to do what you must to earn this remedy?"

"I'm not sure," he admitted. "What do I have to do?"

"Prove yourself a man!" she shouted at him.

"How?"

"There is a monster, conjured by those who do not wish me to live, and I must have its heart if I am to cure you of your condition."

Winslow couldn't believe what she was telling him.

"You mean, if I want to have hair, I have to kill a monster and cut out its heart?"

She nodded her head slowly.

Winslow allowed the thought of this to dwell inside his mind for five seconds before he made hid decision.

"I'll do it," he decided.

Mme. Fortinbras then gave him the details he needed to find his prey. She told him where the wizard who had conjured the creature lived, and what it looked like.

"It is the exact opposite of what you are. Hair covers every inch of its body. It will try to persuade you that it is a harmless man, but do not be fooled. Use this," she said, handing him a long sharp dagger, "to slay it and remove its heart."

Winslow gulped as he looked at the dangerous weapon in his hands. He wondered what he was getting himself into.

"Now go!" she commanded. "Be back before the sun rises or it will be too late!"

A couple of hours later Winslow found himself standing in front of a small quiet house in a secluded suburban neighborhood. His heart thumping like a bass drum in his chest, he knocked timidly on the front door. When there was no response, he tried turning the doorknob to see if the door was locked. It wasn't, and the door opened with a slight squeak.

Holding the dagger in front of him with both hands, he stepped inside the house and nervously made his way through it, searching for any sign of a big hairy monster. Finding nothing on the main floor, he found the door to the basement and went down its rickety wooden steps. In the darkness he could hear the sound of something whimpering. He found the light switch and turned it on. There, in a dark corner on the cement floor, cowered a mass of brown hair.

"Don't believe what she told you," it sobbed out to him as soon as the light came on. "She's lying to you like she lied to me."

"She told me you'd say something like that," Winslow muttered as he moved closer to the pathetic creature.

"She said the same thing to me!" the creature sobbed.

Winslow felt himself hesitate when he got close enough to kill the creature. Why wasn't it putting up a fight? Why was it crying? He found it hard to reconcile the picture of pure evil painted by Mme. Fortinbras with the blubbering brunet mass in front of him. But before sympathy for the creature could soften his heart, he remembered the years of taunts and humiliations he had suffered because he didn't have hair. That was enough for him to drive the dagger deeply into what he assumed was the creature's stomach.

The monster screamed with pain, and Winslow had to stab it repeatedly to get it to stop. Blood spurted everywhere, soaking his clothes and covering the creature's dense thicket of fur. It took him some time to figure out where the creature's heart was, and it took a lot of cutting to get it out of its body. Finally, with the dripping organ in his hand, he ran back upstairs. Needing a place to store it, he found a plastic container in the kitchen. He also found some clothes he could wear in place of his own bloody sweater and jeans.

There was something different about Mme. Fortinbras when he got back to her. She somehow looked older, as if she had aged a decade in just hours. If he were now meeting her for the first time, he would have assumed she was his age, maybe a few years older. He thought about commenting on this, but he stopped himself when it occurred to him that he didn't want to insult her.

"Do you have the heart?" she asked him impatiently.

He handed her the plastic container and she held it carefully in both her hands. She turned away from him and disappeared into one of the small rooms separated by a pile of books. Twenty minutes passed before she appeared again, and Winslow was surprised to find that she now looked just as she had earlier in the day. Something she had done in those 20 minutes had caused 10 years to fade away from her face.

Smiling, she handed him a vial, which contained a warm red potion.

"Drink this as soon as you get home and you will have all the hair you could ever want."

Winslow thanked her for it and rushed out of her apartment. He drove home as fast as he could. He wasn't inside for two seconds before he popped the cork off the vial and swallowed its contents in one long chug. It tasted awful, and he had to fight his own inclination to gag. He ran to the bathroom and stripped off his clothes to take in the full effect. For several long minutes nothing happened, but then—to his amazed delight—hair started to sprout from the top of his head. He shouted with joy as it grew out of him. He looked down and saw hair coming out of his chest and down his arms and legs. He was so happy that he started to cry.

Winslow was so overcome with emotion, it took him a while before he noticed that the hair was still growing. It wasn't stopping. It was sprouting out of his back and all over his face. Every inch of his body was becoming covered with thick brown hair. He grabbed a pair of scissors from the medicine cabinet and started to cut at it, but it was no use. The hair just kept growing.

He looked up from his panic and saw himself in the mirror. To his horror, he found that he looked exactly like the creature he had killed just hours ago. It was then that he realized how big a fool he really was.

He had been so obsessed with his own vanity that he had failed to recognize someone else's. He had found it strange that Mme. Fortinbras went from looking young to middle-aged to young again, but he never asked her how she managed this difficult trick. Now he knew. She did it by fooling hairless suckers like himself and the poor man he'd murdered into supplying her with the fresh human hearts she needed to keep herself young and attractive.

Feeling sick, he collapsed into his empty bathtub and lay there for quite some time. He wondered how long she waited after her special beauty treatments to put another ad in the newspaper. He wondered how long he would have to wait before a bald-headed stranger burst through his door, armed with a sharp dagger to take his heart. He wondered if maybe for all those years that people had made fun of him not because he was bald, but because he was the world's biggest idiot.

Not knowing the answers to any of these questions, he decided that all he could do was wait. He hoped it wouldn't be long.

Straight from the Source

It all depended on who picked the black pearl. All the pledges were blindfolded and made to reach into the skull that had sat on the society's mantelpiece since it was founded, 157 years earlier. Only when all of them had made their selection were they allowed to remove their blindfolds and see who held the black pearl and would have to undergo the sacred Ritual of Rebirth and Renewal. This ritual went back to the earliest days of the society, when its founders decided—after reading Mary Shelley's *Frankenstein*—that the source of all human life was energy and that the quickest way to earn the power that they all craved was to take it directly out of the sky.

They called themselves the Sons of Zeus, and their ranks had included the most successful and powerful men of the past century and a half. Among their current living members were world leaders, owners of international corporations, Nobel Prize winners and men whose fortunes were measured in the billions. Every one of them had reached into that skull when it was his turn, and each had been relieved to find a white pearl in the palm of his hand. They were relieved because they all knew what holding the black pearl could mean.

For 157 years the details of the ritual had remained unchanged, but even a secret society had to occasionally make room for progress. For the first time in the history of the Sons of Zeus, they were allowing for the possibility of a daughter. Leda Swann was the first woman ever to be given an opportunity to pledge the society. Her father was

its most successful member and it was through his influence that she was given this historic chance. Many, however, were not happy about the change and steps were taken to ensure it wouldn't happen again.

As she waited, last in line, Leda could not see that this year the selection process had been rigged against her. Each pledge before her was handed a white pearl and she alone was made to reach into the skull, inside of which sat the lone black pearl.

"Remove your blindfolds," the pledges were ordered by Roberto Jadiz, the society's initiation chairman.

The other pledges pretended to be relieved to find white pearls in their hands, while Leda did her best to stoically accept her duty.

"Pledge Swann," Jadiz walked over to her, "you have chosen the black pearl. Do you know what that means?"

"I do," she answered him as unemotionally as she could.

"Do you understand that if you fail to complete the Ritual of Rebirth and Renewal, you and your fellow pledges will not be allowed to become Sons of Zeus?"

"Yes," she nodded.

"Then come with me, so the ritual can begin."

Jadiz turned and walked through the door that led to the stairs that would take them to the top of the society's headquarters' highest tower. Leda tried not to shake as she turned and followed him. When she was out of earshot the other pledges cheered and celebrated. For their part in the deception against Leda, the society had granted them all membership, regardless of whether or not she completed the ritual. Now, once she failed the test, the society could say that women simply didn't have what it took to be a Son of Zeus and thus avoid a situation like this ever happening again.

It was already raining when Leda and Jadiz climbed through the trapdoor at the end of the stairway and onto the roof of the tower. Two other society members were already there, standing by the large black metal rod that was the centerpiece of the whole ritual. The wind howled past them and Jadiz had to shout to be heard above it.

"The ritual is simple. You are to be chained to this lightning rod from midnight to six o'clock this morning. Placed within your reach is a key that you can use to free yourself, but if you do you fail the ritual. There are only two ways to pass. One is that you last the whole six hours and are still chained to the rod when we come for you in the morning. The other is if the rod is hit by lightning. If that happens, you and your fellow pledges will instantly be accepted into our society." Jadiz allowed a tiny smirk to appear on his face before he continued. "This is the 157th time this ritual has been performed. Before you, 78 pledges have used the key, 52 have lasted the night and 26 have been blessed by lightning. Of those 26, only 3 survived."

With that he nodded to the two others and they led her to the rod and attached manacles to her wrists and ankles. Jadiz showed her the box that contained the key and placed it close enough to her that it would take her no effort at all to retrieve it. Leda maintained her composure right until that moment, when a clap of distant thunder echoed through the wind.

Jadiz and his two henchmen disappeared down the trapdoor and left her alone, chained up in the wind and the rain. The storm was so harsh it made fear of electrocution only a part of the overall torture. Tears came to Leda's eyes as the sharp pellets of rain stung her unprotected skin and soaked her thin initiation cloak. Within a minute her teeth started to chatter as the cold wind headed straight to her bones.

The others sat downstairs and watched, via a hidden rooftop camera, as she suffered in the storm. They laughed and took bets about how long she would last before she went for the key. Most assumed she wouldn't make it for even a few more minutes, much less six more hours, but as the minutes slowly passed, they realized that Leda wasn't going to give in as easily as they had all thought. She was far tougher than they had ever imagined.

As the storm continued to assault her, Leda never once even considered going for the key. Though she was strong and brave and tough, there was another reason keeping her from giving in, and if her initiators had taken a little more time studying the history of their beloved society, they would have known what it was.

Jadiz had memorized the statistics of the Ritual so he could use them to psych out all those who were chained to the rod, but in the four years he had served as the society's initiation chairman he had never bothered to look up the names of the three men who had survived when they were hit by lightning. If he had, he would have learned that the last time a pledge was struck and lived was 35 years ago, and that that pledge's name was Anderson Swann. Anderson was Leda's father, the man who had used his power and influence to ensure that she would be the first woman to pledge the society. Not only did he know that the others would cheat to make sure his daughter was forced to undergo the ritual, he had actually counted on it. The night before he had explained his reasons to his daughter.

"I was never more afraid than I was that night," he had admitted to her. "I knew that the year before, a pledge had been killed in the very spot where I stood and every part of me wanted to go for the key. The great stupidity of the whole enterprise astounded me and I couldn't understand what was keeping me from giving in. Perhaps I was afraid that failing there would be the first step in a whole lifetime of failure, or that I would disappoint my father, who was a member. Whatever the reason, I stayed, and the longer I stayed, the angrier I became. I started to hate these men who pretended to believe in the society's ancient mysticisms, but who really were members only because the society enabled them to network with the world's elite. They claimed they were Sons of Zeus, but they were really only the Sons of Power." Leda's father paused for a moment, as he felt the pleasure that came from recalling an important epiphany. "It was at that moment that I felt it! The electricity—*the power*—surged through me and I saw him. I saw Zeus! And he spoke to me. He told me that he was tired of having his name blasphemed by these fools and that he had waited for a man to be chained to the rod who understood the folly of their existence. It would be my duty to help set in motion the events that would lead to the end of the society and the downfall of all those who benefited from it. He told me that I would have a daughter"—at this, Leda's father had smiled at her—"and that she would be the one who destroyed the Sons of Zeus for once and for all!"

As the rain slashed across her face, Leda remembered those words and understood why these sadistic men had to be stopped. Since the society had been founded, 24 men had died so the spoiled sons of wealthy fathers could meet and plan how to best exploit the world for their benefit. It was then, at that moment, that she felt the power surge through her body.

The men watching downstairs panicked when they saw the rooftop camera cut out just as the lightning struck the rod. None of the members in attendance were even born the last time a pledge was killed during the ritual and they were ill prepared to deal with it. Jadiz and his henchmen ran up to the roof, only to find—as they climbed through the trapdoor—a smiling Leda, calmly unlocking herself from her chains.

"How—" Jadiz stuttered when he saw her.

Leda turned toward him. She laughed and looked up at the sky and snapped her fingers. At once, the rain stopped falling and the wind stopped howling. Though it was dark outside, the three men could hardly look at her, her skin being so radiant it shone like a beacon. She stepped toward them, and with each step the building rocked. When she spoke to them, the voice that came out was Leda's, but it had in it a quality of confidence and power they had never heard before.

"You don't need to know how," she told him. "It is enough for you to know that it has happened and that Zeus has spoken to me. He had something he wanted me to pass on to you." Her smile turned into a smirk as she continued. "He says, 'Watch your backs.'"

The three men stared at her without comprehension as she turned and ran and jumped off the top of the tower. When she was gone they ran over to the edge to see where she had fallen, but her body was nowhere in sight.

From that day on the members of the society watched helplessly as their fortunes turned. Those who were politicians found that the scandals they had successfully kept hidden were now all being discovered. Those who owned corporations saw their companies go bankrupt or bought out by Anderson Swann, the only member who seemed unaffected by the apparent curse. The society's wealthiest members watched as the sources of their wealth dried up and their possessions were destroyed in a rash of fires that plagued their homes. To their stunned horror they were told by the insurance companies they used to own that their policies were worthless. It was clear to them that something or someone was behind their cataclysmic bad luck, but they did not know who or what it was.

Jadiz and his two henchmen could not tell them. After seeing Leda fly off the roof of the tower, they found themselves unable to communicate in any way. They had been found lying on the tower's roof, their hair turned white and their eyes bugged out in terror.

Not long after, Anderson Swann retired and made his daughter the CEO of his enormous company. Those who met her were awed by her charisma and the power she exuded. Some went so far as to claim that whenever she walked, they could feel the ground shake. Hearing people say that always made her smile.

The House Sitter

Arthur always found it difficult getting used to a new bed. Just a few days before, he had been sleeping on a lumpy futon, which—thanks to Flufster, his roommate's pet cat—always smelled a little funny, and he missed it. Sure, it was uncomfortable and the futon smelled bad, but his body understood it and knew how to lie on it for a good night's sleep. This new bed was huge and immaculate and it smelled of freshly laundered goodness and he couldn't get a wink of sleep on it no matter how hard he tried.

He lay awake in the bed's expensive fine cotton sheets and stared up at the white lace canopy above him. The whole situation struck him as odd. It was hard to believe that he was attempting to rest in a bedroom whose furniture cost more than he had earned in the past five years. In fact, the events that had led him to this moment had gone by so fast that he decided that this was a good opportunity to stop and try to work out in his head what had actually happened.

It all started when his cousin Trisha called him. This, in itself, was weird, since she had never called him before in his entire life. He and Trisha were so completely different that they usually didn't even talk to each other the few times of the year their family gathered, much less when circumstances didn't force them to meet. She was a no-nonsense, nose-to-the-grindstone type who had married Todd, a similarly inclined corporate go-getter, and they weren't inclined to associate with the kind of bohemian slackers who considered Arthur their king. On the phone she had sounded anxious.

"I'm sorry to bother you, Arthur," she had apologized, "but I have no one else to turn to. You're my last resort."

Some people might have been offended by this remark, but Arthur shrugged it off. It wasn't the first time someone in his family had said it to him.

"Whaddaya need?" he asked her.

"Me and Todd are both going to be away on business trips starting tomorrow and we need someone to look after the house while we're gone."

"I thought you guys had a maid?"

Trisha paused for a second before she answered him. "She quit and we don't have time in our schedules to hire someone new until we get back."

"So what would I have to do?"

"Just the usual household duties. Take in the paper and the mail, water the plants, feed our dog Nelson, turn on the security alarms at night and—" she added one more chore, but she mumbled it so he didn't understand her.

"What was that last one?" he asked her.

"Turn on the security alarms at night," she repeated.

"No, you said something after that."

"I'm sorry Arthur, but you're breaking up. I think my cell phone battery is low. Can you help us or not?"

Arthur looked around his apartment. It was filthy. His roommate, Jed, was zoned out in front of a violent videogame and Flufster was licking a congealed liquid out of a dish that had been in the sink for three weeks. Upstairs one of his neighbors was apparently attempting to learn how to play the bagpipes and it sounded as if the police were making a spirited surprise visit to the couple that lived next door.

"Yeah, I guess I can make it," he answered her.

"Great," she said just before her phone cut them off.

A minute later he was on his way to her house. Even though he had only been there once before, when she and Todd had hosted Christmas one year, he had no trouble finding it. It was the only house on its block with pillars framing its front door and the only one with a $90,000 European sports car in its driveway. His own car—which he had bought for $625—sputtered to a stop in front of their sidewalk, and he took a look in his rearview mirror to make sure there weren't any potato chip crumbs in his beard. Satisfied that he looked presentable, he hopped out of his junker and rang the doorbell. An exasperated Todd answered, barely giving Arthur a nod as he shouted instructions into a cordless phone.

Arthur walked in and found the front room to be even more impressive without an intricately decorated pine tree inside it. Todd had disappeared, so Arthur sat down on the sofa and rifled through a coffee table book about the Amazon that was heavier and more expensive than most coffee tables.

"Arthur, Hi," Trisha said when she appeared from the kitchen. "Glad that you can help us out on such short notice. Vera...uh...quit a week ago and I wouldn't have known what to do if you weren't available."

"Happy to help," Arthur shrugged.

For the next half hour Trisha showed him around the house and told him everything he had to do. She introduced him to Nelson, their Jack Russell terrier, who seemed a lot nicer than Flufster, and she told him that he was welcome to help himself to any of the food in their fridge or freezer and to the wine in their cellar. Around the end of the tour, she became distracted as though there was one last thing she wanted to tell him but was reluctant to. Whatever it was, she decided to keep it to herself.

Both Trisha and Todd had to get up early to leave the next morning, so they went to bed at nine o'clock, leaving Arthur to play with their mammoth home entertainment system before he went to bed in their guest room, with its huge canopy bed.

Having worked out how he had gotten there, he still couldn't get to sleep. The house creaked and moaned, like any other building during the silence of the night. Around four, he heard Trisha and Todd rouse themselves out of bed, and they left for the airport an hour later.

He was now officially alone.

Trisha and Todd weren't gone for three seconds before Nelson started passionately barking at something downstairs, which was unfortunate since Arthur at that point had almost managed to fall asleep. His eyes popped open and he sighed the sigh of the inconvenienced before he got out of bed to investigate the cause of the pooch's loud yaps. Dressed only in his boxers, he yawned as he walked downstairs and turned toward the kitchen. There he saw the tiny dog apparently confronting an intruder who was standing out of sight. Smoke drifted out into the hallway, and the air smelled like cheap cigarettes.

Arthur turned into the front room, grabbed the heavy book from the coffee table and held it up above his head,

assuming that it was more than solid enough to knock out whoever was being barked at. Slowly he made his way toward Nelson, until he was just a few feet away, then he jumped with a loud scream, seeing for the first time who was causing this commotion.

Arthur screamed, partly because he dropped the book on his left foot, and partly because he was not used to seeing the ghost of a small woman in her early 60s. Disturbed by his screams, the ghost began to scream as well, which, along with Nelson's continued barking, made for a lot of noise. Finally, it became so absurd that they all stopped, except for Nelson, who would not be deterred.

It was Arthur who broke the tension by speaking first.

"Shut up, Nelson!" he shouted at the small dog, which looked up at him and stopped barking.

"Thanks," sighed the ghost, her voice tinged with the rasp of a lifelong smoker, "stupid little thing was driving me batty."

"Don't mention it," Arthur shrugged. He then took a moment before he felt comfortable enough to ask the obvious question. "So, you're, like, a ghost, right?"

"That's right," she nodded.

"Funny. Trisha didn't mention that this place was haunted," he explained.

"I think she left you a note," the ghost said, pointing to a piece of stationery left on the kitchen table.

Arthur walked over and picked it up and read it.

Dear Arthur,
    I should have told you sooner, but I think our house is haunted. If it helps, I've only noticed

the ghost over the past few days and it seems to be harmless, despite the fact that it smells like unfiltered menthols.

Sorry,
Trisha

"So I guess you haven't been here that long," Arthur said to the ghost when he finished reading it.

"Just a week now. You can call me Vera, by the way."

"Hi Vera, I'm Arthur." He introduced himself politely with a wave, assuming she was too immaterial for a handshake. He was about to say something else when a thought occurred to him. "There's a coincidence," he spoke aloud, "Trisha and Todd had a maid named Vera."

"I know," the ghost nodded.

Arthur did the arithmetic in his mind. "That's not a coincidence, is it?" he asked.

Vera shook her head, which looked weird since it caused wisps of white smoke to float out into the air. "Nope," she admitted.

"Trisha said you had quit a week ago," he told her.

"Well, that is what Todd told her."

"Why would he do that?"

"Because he killed me."

It took a second before Arthur fully comprehended this unexpected revelation.

"Oh," was what he said when he finally understood.

"Although I'm pretty sure she doesn't believe him," she added. "Her having seen me and all."

"Have you spoken with her?" asked Arthur.

"Haven't had the chance. I'm new to this whole spirit world thing, but I guess it takes a couple of days before a ghost becomes strong enough to communicate with the living. You're the first person I've talked to since I died."

"Why did Todd kill you?" he asked her.

"Oh, I overheard him talking on the phone about his plan to kill Trisha for her life insurance money. Apparently it's the only way he'll be able to afford to keep that stupid car in the driveway."

"What did he do to you?"

"Hit me over the head with that book you just dropped on your toe. Then he buried me in the small crawl space under the house."

"So is that why you're here?" he asked her. "To make sure I prevent Todd from killing my cousin?"

"No, it's more of a personal vengeance thing," Vera admitted. "Don't get me wrong, I'm *against* the idea of Todd killing someone else, but—having worked for her—I wouldn't be *too* choked up if Trisha kicked the bucket. There's a word for what she is, but I'm far too old-fashioned to use it."

Arthur understood what Vera meant. Having spent a dozen childhood summer vacations with his cousin, he had long ago come to the same conclusion.

"Still, I should do something about it," he decided. "If only for my Auntie Susan."

"Hey," Vera shrugged, "as long as I get some justice, I don't care what you do."

"Cool," said Arthur. Then, with a yawn, he picked up the heavy book from the kitchen floor. "It was nice to meet you, Vera," he said politely, "but I need to get some sleep, so I'll see you later today."

"That's fine," said Vera, "I'm not going anywhere."

Arthur put the book back on the coffee table and then went back to bed. By then he was so tired he could have slept on a bed of nails and not been bothered by it. When he woke up he realized that what had happened just six hours earlier was so odd that he might have only dreamed it.

Still dressed in just his boxers, he walked downstairs and was immediately hit by the pungent odor of thick cigarette smoke.

"Hi, Arthur," Vera greeted him, her smoky shape hovering in front of a soap opera on Trisha and Todd's 32-inch plasma TV.

Arthur—still operating on the dream theory—screamed again, then apologized.

"Sorry. I wasn't expecting you."

"Don't worry about it," Vera laughed, "I'm guessing it comes with the ghost territory."

From that point on, the two became friends, and over the next four days, they brainstormed ways in which they could foil Todd's plans to murder his wife while also seeing him punished for Vera's murder. While Arthur preferred the idea of simply informing the police, Vera insisted it had to be something more dramatic.

"I came back from the dead for this," she reasoned. "You can't expect my soul to be satisfied by him being dragged off to some prison. Where's the fun in that? I say we drop his precious car off a cliff while he's in it. There's your—whatchamacallit—cosmic justice."

In the end, after much deliberation, they came up with a plan they both liked.

"And then finally we get him to set his car on fire," Vera repeated as they went over the scheme one last time.

"Right," Arthur nodded, "but only after he's eaten the life insurance policy."

"Sounds like a winner to me," she said, smiling, before something caught her attention. "Did you hear that?" she asked him.

"No, what was it?"

"I don't know, it sounded like a footstep."

"It's probably just Nelson."

"Yeah, I guess. What time was Todd supposed to be coming home?" she asked.

"Nine, unless his meeting ended at noon, which meant he would be getting an earlier flight."

"Which means..."

"He could have got in half an hour ago!" said Arthur as he jumped up out of his chair.

"Which means..."

"He heard everything!"

"Damn it!" Vera swore as she quickly hovered up through the ceiling to the second floor to see if he was there.

Arthur listened carefully for any sound that might indicate Todd's presence in the house. Slowly, he walked out of the den and down the hallway toward the front room, grabbing a poker from the fireplace as he moved. Wielding it like a baseball bat, he kept his eyes open, but not open enough.

"Ow," he whimpered when he felt a large heavy object hit him in the back of his head. Dropping the poker, he fell to the floor and felt his consciousness leave his body as the blunt instrument was repeatedly slammed against the back of his skull.

Vera had been right; it took a few days for a ghost to fully materialize. All Arthur could do was watch as Vera's vengeful spirit did her best to harass Todd. Because she was just a harmless wisp of a phantom, the unflappable yuppie ignored her and carried out his plans to murder Trisha. Not wanting Vera to warn her, Todd picked his wife up from the airport and drove her to a deserted warehouse and performed the foul deed there. Vera and Arthur tried to follow him, but they both found they could not leave the house. Just as Arthur was becoming whole enough to speak, he and Vera were joined by Trisha's understandably perturbed wraith. Together the three ghosts watched as Todd placed his wife's dead body into their bed and calmly set their house on fire, only to drive away in his treasured automobile.

It was then that Arthur's ghost was finally able to speak.

"You two wouldn't happen to know what happens to us when there's no house anymore, do you?"

Vera didn't know, and Trisha hadn't been dead long enough to answer him even if she did.

As the flames ate away at the house, Arthur decided then and there that sometimes it was a mistake to help someone out just because they were family.

Building a Family

The first thing Sal noticed about his new workmate at the meat processing plant was that he sure did like to talk about his family. Ernie was a tall, thin man in his late 50s who refused to be deterred from his nonstop monologues by the plant's rapid—sometimes dangerous—pace and the constant roar of its machinery. He talked *a lot*, about *many* things, but mostly he talked about his family. By the end of their first shift together, Sal had heard so much about them he could tell you their names, ages, favorite sports, food preferences and personal pet peeves. Truthfully, he wasn't interested in any of these details, but being just 18 and fresh out of high school he was still uncomfortable with the idea of telling an older person to shut up.

So, as the weeks and months went by, he heard more and more about Ernie's family. He heard all about their birthday parties, new hobbies, fights and everything else the older man believed to be worthy of an anecdote (his standards being much lower than most). Occasionally Sal would grow annoyed by Ernie's endless prattling, but he was always too busy to complain, and he tried his best to just ignore him.

To Ernie—who had grown used to being insulted and shouted at for his constant talking—Sal's silence was a clear indication that the boy was interested in everything he had to say, so he made sure to never run out of good stories to tell. Some days, when he couldn't think of anything that had really happened, he would just make stuff up. He worried that some of these stories might sound a bit too farfetched (like the one about his daughter winning the local junior miss beauty pageant) but Sal never questioned them. Having lived his life only ever wanting a good audience, Ernie grew to really like the boy, and he tried to mentor him in the ways of meat processing the best he could.

But this was only a summer job for Sal, a way to save up tuition money for the local college he would attend that fall, so he had no real use for Ernie's sage career counseling. He never said this to Ernie, not wanting to hurt his feelings, but a lot of the time the constant stream of well-meaning advice got on his nerves. And it would have irritated Sal even if he had been interested in meat processing. Ernie had worked in the same spot in the plant for over 20 years, a clear indication to Sal that his supposed mentor was not proficient enough to be promoted, but just good enough to avoid being fired. It was like getting career advice about becoming an executive from someone who had never left the mailroom.

Still, Sal tried not to give the pathetic older man a hard time, if only because Ernie was usually so cheerful and happy, which made him a real rarity in the plant. Having grown used to Ernie's friendly demeanor, Sal was surprised to find it gone on the first morning of his last week at the plant before school started. As he watched his usually effusive coworker toil silently beside him, he found it strangely unsettling. Normally he would have been thrilled to go a whole shift without Ernie saying a word, but not when it was so obvious that the man was genuinely unhappy. Sal's concern grew until he finally broke down and did the unthinkable. He asked Ernie what was wrong. Expecting to be thrown off his feet by a deluge of information, he was surprised when Ernie just shrugged and mumbled something so quietly it couldn't be heard above the noise of the machines.

"What was that?" asked Sal.

Ernie mumbled again, but this time just loud enough to be heard.

"Donnie's not doing too well." Donnie was his oldest son, close to Sal's age.

"What's wrong?"

"He just can't keep his head on straight."

"He'll grow out of that," Sal reassured him.

"I don't think so," Ernie said dolefully, shaking his head. "I'm going to have to do something about it."

"Like what?"

"I don't know yet, but I'll think of something."

Sal could tell that Ernie didn't want him to press the issue, so he left it at that. Ernie remained depressed for the rest of the week, until the Friday that was Sal's last day on the job.

"Y'know," Ernie smiled at Sal, "you're a kid with a good head on his shoulders."

"Thanks," said Sal.

"I think Donnie could really benefit from meeting a kid as put together as you. I wish you could meet him."

"Yeah, me too."

"Really?"

"Uh, sure."

"Well, why don't you come over to the house after work?" Ernie asked.

Sal hadn't seen this one coming.

"I dunno," he demurred.

"Come on! It'll be fun. After all this time you have to be dying to meet my family in person."

Dying wasn't the word Sal would have used, but Ernie wouldn't give up until he agreed to come over for dinner that night. After their shift was over, they both climbed out of their stained white overalls and smocks and cleaned themselves up before heading out. They got into Ernie's old wreck of a car and headed to his house out in the suburbs.

Ernie was back to his usual talkative self, and Sal sat and wondered how he had gotten roped into this situation. As of today he was officially free from the meat processing plant, hopefully never to return, so why was he going to visit the family of the guy who had annoyed him daily over the past few months? He cursed himself for being too polite. A less considerate man would have just told Ernie the truth, that he had no desire whatsoever to meet the sad man's family, but because he was foolish enough to worry about Ernie's feelings he was going to have to endure what he knew would be an excruciating evening.

As they drove up Ernie's driveway, Sal noted that his house was just as big a dump as he had expected. The paint was peeling off the house's facade, and the ground was covered with roof shingles that had blown off during the previous night's rainstorm. Before they walked inside, Sal got a clear mental picture of faded and peeling '70s-era wallpaper and ratty furniture. His vision proved to be so embarrassingly accurate, Sal briefly wondered if he was psychic.

As they stood in the doorway, Ernie turned and spoke to Sal.

"There's something about my family I never told you," he whispered.

Sal found that *very* hard to believe.

"What?" he asked.

Ernie closed the door behind them and locked it.

"They're not like a normal family," he explained.

"I kinda gathered that," Sal gently teased.

"No, really. They're very different."

Sal was about to say something when Ernie's wife, Estelle, came in from the kitchen to greet them.

"Hi, guys," she said cheerfully.

Sal screamed. He didn't mean to, but he screamed very loudly.

A person could tell that Estelle had once been a beauty, but the effects of time had taken their toll on her face. In her case, however, wrinkles were not the problem. It was that her nose had fallen off.

Sal's screams startled her and she raised her hand to her face. It was then that she noticed something was wrong.

"It came off again," she sighed wearily. "That glue you bought just won't hold it in place," she scolded Ernie.

"That's what I get for buying the cheap stuff," Ernie chided himself.

Sal had stopped screaming. He would have felt incredibly guilty for his bad manners had it been clear that Estelle's lack of nose was the result of a birth defect, accident or leprosy, but he didn't because it was obvious that she was a corpse. He had seen enough zombie movies in his youth to know how to recognize a member of the walking dead.

Candy, Ernie's teenage daughter, came down the stairs, causing Sal to scream once again.

"What's his problem?" she asked her father, as she picked an annoying maggot off her rotting face.

Sal turned toward the door to get out, only to find that the lock Ernie had used required a combination to open it.

"Where you going, buddy?" Ernie threw an unwelcome arm around Sal's shoulders. "You have to meet Donnie. That's why you're here, after all."

Sal did not want to meet Donnie. He wanted to jump out of the closest window and escape from this madness, but as he scanned the living room he saw that all the windows were boarded shut.

"Is this the guy you were telling me about?" Sal heard someone say. He looked up and nearly fainted. Standing in front of him was a teenage boy whose neck was broken and incapable of holding up his head. This had to be Donnie.

"Sure is," beamed Ernie.

This proved too much for Sal to take. He fainted dead away and landed hard on the floor. When he came to a few minutes later, he could not move. He was strapped onto a soiled cot, with a swath of duct tape covering his mouth and rendering him unable to speak. Ernie, Estelle, Donnie and Candy all stood over him.

"I know I'm not so hot when it comes to meat processing," Ernie admitted to his struggling captive, "but I'm aces when it comes to voodoo. Isn't that right, kids?"

"That's right, Dad," Donnie and Candy chorused.

"Y'see, Sal, I used to be real lonely. I lived by myself and I couldn't seem to find anybody to start a family with, so I decided to do the next best thing. I built one myself!"

"Pffmmfmfmmfmmmfmm?" asked Sal.

"Oh, it was easy. I just went to the library and studied old newspaper obituaries. When I saw one for somebody I thought I could live with, I dug them up and performed the standard zombie rites. No big deal, really. Obviously I started with Estelle here, because I wanted my kids to have a mother. We had Donnie after that, and Candy's the youngest, which is ironic since she died before I was born."

"Pfmfmpppppfmmfpppfmmmmmmf!" Sal shouted accusingly.

"I am not crazy!" Ernie defended himself. "Is it crazy to want a family? I don't think so. If I'm crazy, then 90 percent of America is out to lunch!"

"Pfffffffmmmmfmfmfmmffmghgh," pleaded Sal.

"I would love to let you go, but we have a problem. As you can see, one of the downfalls of building your own family is that every now and then they fall apart and you have to fix them up. You saw how Estelle's nose had fallen off, and how Donnie's neck can't hold up his head anymore. A lot of times all I need to get the job done is some surgical thread and strong glue, but in big cases, like Donnie's here, I need a replacement part. I told you that you had a good head on your shoulders, and even though I admit this is probably somewhat inconvenient for you, I'm going to have to borrow it."

Sal began to scream, but the sound of his terror was muted by the duct tape.

"Don't be like that," Ernie scolded him gently. "You'll like being a part of our family. It's a lot of fun, isn't it, kids?"

"Sure is!" agreed Donnie and Candy.

"And you get used to feeling dead," added Estelle. "It's nowhere near as bad as you might think."

Sal screamed and struggled as hard as he could to escape from his bonds, but they were too tight.

Ernie shook his head sadly. "Looks like he isn't going to be too helpful, is he, kids," he sighed.

"Nope," they agreed with him.

"That's too bad. Candy, get me one of the cyanide syringes, and Donnie, start up the chainsaw."

Sal fought them with all his might, but to no avail. Candy jabbed him roughly with a needle and seconds later Sal felt his life ebb out of him. Luckily, he was dead by the time Donnie got the chainsaw working.

It took Ernie a couple of hours to make the switch of heads and perform the ritual to reawaken his son. Donnie's eyes opened and, still groggy, he asked his dad for a mirror so he could check out his new head. Ernie handed one over and Donnie looked into it.

"Whaddya think, kiddo?" Ernie asked with a smile.

Donnie studied his new face. It would take him a while to get used to seeing Sal's features in his reflection, but he really liked them.

"I love it, Dad," Donnie beamed. "You were right. This one was perfect for me."

"I'm glad to hear it," grinned Ernie. "Now do me a favor and put the rest of Sal's body into the freezer. You never know when we're going to need more parts."

Three Simple Words

Ever since she was a young girl, the only thing Angela D'Erricho wanted was someone to love. Anyone who spent even 10 minutes with her would assume she would have no trouble making her dream come true, as she was an uncommonly beautiful woman with a charming sense of humor and a generous and caring personality. But despite her good looks and sunny disposition, she was destined—thanks to a childhood prank she had nothing to do with and the Old World fury of an angry grandmother—to spend most of her life alone.

It all started in the eighth grade, when Angela was that rare student who managed to be both popular *and* well liked. An early bloomer, she had by the age of 13 already developed the body she would wear as an adult, and as a result she was greatly admired by the boys of her school. Despite her physical maturity, she was too young emotionally to be aware of the effect she had on others. It had yet to occur to her that many people were nice to her for reasons other than simple friendliness, and she would have been shocked to discover that she was a constant fixture in the daydreams of many of her peers.

One of these daydreamers was a quiet boy named Adrian. Short and slight, he was often the target of the school's resident bullies, who took sport in thinking up ways to mistreat him. One day, one of these bullies—a heavyset oaf named Neil—caught Adrian looking too long in Angela's direction during lunch. As dense as Neil was, even he was able to sense the longing in Adrian's eyes, and he saw in them a chance to have some fun. When he told his friends about Adrian's obvious crush, they all immediately decided to exploit Adrian's feelings for their own amusement.

To do this they got their friend Tabitha, who was an excellent forger of other people's handwriting, to write a note to Adrian. Supposedly from Angela, the note was a declaration of love, and it requested that Adrian meet her after school in the girls' bathroom beside the seventh-grade science room. When Tabitha finished writing it, Neil slipped it into Adrian's locker, giggling cruelly at the thought of what was to come.

Adrian couldn't believe his eyes when he opened his locker and the note floated out to his feet. He trembled as he picked it up and read it. He had been the victim of many similar pranks, and part of him couldn't help suspecting that the note was a fake, meant to lure him into another humiliating situation. But another part of him, the one responsible for reams of bad poetry about the girl of his dreams, wanted to believe—against all reason—that it was real. As he stood and pondered the note, risking being late for his next class, he looked up and saw Angela walk by. She smiled at him, and this was enough for him to conclude that the note must be genuine.

The truth was that Angela hadn't smiled *at* Adrian; he had merely looked up when she had a smile on her face, which was a pretty common occurrence for a happy person such as Angela. Though she would never know it, that smile would—in the end—lead to the curse that would ruin her life.

A few hours later, Adrian hesitated outside the girls' bathroom. Of course he was nervous about entering, not just because he might be walking into a trap, but also because it was *the girls' bathroom*. This was the forbidden zone into which no boy was supposed to pass. Being caught inside not only could lead to detention, it could also mean giving the school's bullies another round of ammo to aim in his direction. "Hey, Adrienne," he could hear them call him (it really didn't help that his name could be so easily converted into the feminine), "whatcha doin' in the boys' bathroom? Don't you know that girls like you can't come in here?" But, after taking a moment to build up his courage, he risked all these dangers and walked into the bathroom.

As soon as he was inside, Neil and two other boys cackled like hyenas as they grabbed him and lifted him off the ground. Adrian struggled and tried to fight his way out of their grasp, but they were too strong for him. He shouted angrily as they led him to a bathroom stall, and he kicked at them as hard as he could as they lowered his head into the toilet. Neil flushed it repeatedly as the other two boys laughed so hard they almost lost their grip. Adrian thrashed and cried and gasped for air, but he only became free when the three boys lifted him back up and dumped him onto the hard, cold tile floor.

"Loser," Neil insulted him with a laugh as he and his cohorts left him alone to cry.

More humiliated than he ever had been before, Adrian finally got up and trudged home. He lived only a short distance away, so as he walked into his family's kitchen, his hair and clothes were still soaking wet. Both of his parents worked, but his elderly grandmother, who lived with them, was there cooking a stew for dinner.

"What happened to you?" she asked him in her thick Russian accent.

Not one to hide the truth from his family, he told her. As she listened, his grandmother—who had grown up in a small village where the old ways had never died—grew more and more angry. As angry as she was at the boys who had flushed her beloved grandson's head in the toilet, the person she was angriest at was the girl who had lured him into this trap. Despite Adrian's protests that Angela probably had nothing to do with the prank, she went downstairs to the room no one else was allowed to enter and conjured up a curse against Angela—a curse so cruel it made Adrian's toilet dunking look like an act of charity in comparison.

"For she who would use love against an innocent like Adrian," she incanted over an evil-smelling concoction of herbs and other ingredients, "let her now know the pain that can be caused by love. Let her know the burning that comes from desire!"

Completely unaware of what was happening, Angela was at home playing with her Barbie dolls. Though she looked like a young woman, she was still very much a young girl and she loved playing with the toys of her childhood. For what must have been the thousandth time, Ken and Barbie were getting married. They had just exchanged rings and kissed each other when Angela, speaking for Barbie, said to Ken, "I love you."

The words were not one second out of her mouth when the male doll heated up and began to smoke right

there in her hand. She dropped it to the floor and watched, amazed, as it burst into flames in front of her. She grabbed a blanket from her bed and used it to smother the flames. When they were out she sat down on the floor and tried to figure out what had just happened. Not being sure at all, she placed the other doll in front of her on the floor and spoke to it. "I love you, Barbie," she whispered hesitantly.

To her astonishment this caused the other doll to also burst into flames. She quickly smothered the fire and stood up and—panicked by what was happening—tried it again to make sure she wasn't crazy. She looked at the poster beside her on the wall. It was a picture of a teenage boy named Drake Benson, who starred on her favorite television show, *This Is My World*.

"I love you, Drake," she said to it and watched with relief as it failed to ignite. She breathed out a heavy sigh and started to clean up the mess made by the burning dolls. Thanks to the melted plastic, this task took a lot longer than she expected. She had been at it for an hour when her mother called up to her from downstairs. "Angela, come here," she shouted, "there's something happening on TV."

Curious, Angela ran downstairs, and her heart almost stopped beating when she saw what had happened. There on the news was the hour-old footage of a bizarre accident that had just occurred on the set of America's favorite sitcom. Caught by the studio's cameras during a rehearsal was the horrible sight of teen heartthrob Drake Benson bursting into a bright orange flame. It had taken the stunned crew half a minute before someone had the sense to try to extinguish him, but by then it was too late. Drake had burned to death.

Angela collapsed right there on the floor of her parents' living room, her body unable to properly process the horror of what she had somehow caused. Tears began to flood out of her eyes as a horrible combination of grief and guilt hit her like a cannonball in the solar plexus. Her parents tried to calm her, but her sobs grew so heavy she started to hyperventilate. Not knowing what else to do, they called an ambulance.

She was given a sedative at the hospital, and that was enough to calm her down. A psychologist was brought in to ask her some questions. Angela told him that seeing Drake go up in flames was what had caused her to become hysterical, but she was smart enough not to mention that she was the one who was actually responsible for the accident. She was fully aware of how crazy that would sound to a doctor who specialized in figuring out if someone was crazy or not. Luckily, the doctor bought her explanation, and she was released from the hospital a few hours later.

Angela knew there was no one she could talk to about what had happened. Still incapable of believing it herself, she aimed the cursed phrase at a handful of disposable objects until she finally convinced herself that anything she expressed love for would immediately burst into flames. She didn't even have to speak the words, as they had the same effect when she wrote them down.

Almost immediately she started to treat people differently. She became less open and tried hard never to form friendships. Incapable of being rude or obnoxious, she instead stayed as quiet as she could and made every attempt to shun the closeness of others. She withdrew from her family and gave away all her pets, for fear the words might slip out one day accidentally.

The years passed and Angela graduated from high school, marked with the reputation of a pretty girl who thought too much of herself to associate with others. As much as she hated people thinking of her that way, she knew it was for the best. The more they hated her, the easier it would be for her not to become attached.

She went to college, where she studied English. Tormented by her loneliness, she began to turn her pain into short stories. Based on the advice of a kind teacher, whom she tried very hard to dislike, she started to send her stories to publishers. Within a couple of years she was working full-time as a writer.

Writing was perfect for her, because she could do it from home and deal with her editors and publishers by phone, fax or e-mail. The lonelier she got, the more she wrote. Her books were very popular and she received hundreds of fan letters a week. She never read any of them. Instead she just pushed them down her apartment building's garbage chute into the furnace. She never gave interviews and refused to have her picture published anywhere, which only helped to make her more famous. Millions of people who never would have otherwise heard of her knew her as that reclusive, eccentric author who never left her apartment, even to buy groceries.

Fans of her books tried every trick they could to meet her, but—even if they got past the large doorman in the lobby—she opened her door to no one, not even members of her own family.

Angela had gone almost a decade without seeing another person when her intercom buzzed loudly one quiet afternoon. The buzzer set off a message she had taped years and years ago, in which she told the caller that she was not expecting any visitors and that she could not make herself available at this time. The problem with the message was that, even after years of solitude, she had never been able to lose her natural politeness, which made her words sound forced and unconvincing. Despite the sincerity of her words, the tone of her voice gave people the impression that she wasn't serious and that she would just love to have someone come in and visit her, so inevitably they would press the buzzer again and again until she answered in person.

"Go away," she sighed into it this particular afternoon.

"Angela!" the other voice exclaimed. "You have to let me in!"

"No, I don't," she sighed.

"I know all about your problem," the voice insisted.

Over the years many of her fans had come to believe that they had figured out—through reading her work— the cause of her neurosis and that they could help her if she just let them into her life.

"Just leave me alone," she pleaded.

"Listen to me!" The voice's urgency was not masked by the hiss of the intercom's cheap speakers. "I can make it so you can tell people you love them again!"

Angela's heart skipped a beat.

"W-w-hat did you say?" she asked, her voice shaking.

"I can lift the curse!"

Stunned and confused, she turned away from the intercom and slowly made her way to the door. She unlocked and opened it, revealing a short, skinny man about her age. She looked at him and dimly recognized a face from a long time ago.

"Angela," the man explained, "you probably don't remember me, but my name is Adrian Tarkovski. We went to school together. It's because of me that you're cursed."

All Angela could do was stare at him. If what he said was true, then she had every right to scream and throw herself at him with a fury fired by the anguish of 20 years of self-enforced isolation. But instead, she just stepped aside and gave him the space he needed to come in.

As soon as he was in, words flowed out of his mouth in a torrent. He told her everything. He told her about the prank and how just a month earlier his grandmother had finally died at the age of 103, and that as he was going through her belongings, he found her diary, and there he read about what she had done to Angela. He explained to her that the old woman had taught him some of the old ways and that he was certain he could reverse the curse.

Angela showed no emotion as she listened to him. When he finished, she asked him what she had to do.

"Nothing," he told her. "I do all the work."

"Then get to it."

With that he ran back downstairs and retrieved his supplies. He set everything up carefully in her small kitchen and worked steadily, brewing a noxious combination of herbs and other ingredients. He spoke aloud the incantation he had found in one of his grandmother's old books. Finally, after two hours, he looked up at Angela and shrugged.

"I think that's it," he told her.

"I don't feel any different," she said.

"The only way we can find out is if you say it."

"I don't know if I can," she admitted to him. "It's been so long."

"Yes, you can. Say it to me."

"But what if it didn't work?"

"Then I get what I deserve. It's because of me you're trapped in this prison. If what you went through is even one tiny bit as bad as I imagine, then I deserve to burn."

"That's not true."

"Yes, it is, and you know it."

"I can't do it!"

"Yes, you can!"

"I can't!"

"ANGELA, SAY IT!"

"Adrian, I love you!" The words leapt out of her mouth before she could stop them. She closed her eyes and fell to the floor, terrified by what she might have caused. She started to cry, but before the grief overcame her she felt her hands being lifted away from her face. Adrian stood before her with a smile. Tears continued to stream down her face as she stared at him.

"You're still here," she marveled.

"Yes, I am," he grinned.

Still crying, she hugged him as tightly as she could and told him that she loved him over and over again, the words sounding more wonderful every time she said them. Adrian hugged her back and remembered how he had felt about her all those years ago. He discovered that those feelings had never gone away. Caught in the exhilaration of the moment, he found himself saying the words he had wanted to say for so many years.

"Angela, I love you, too."

Angela suddenly stopped and let go of him. She stepped away, and Adrian felt like a fool for revealing his feelings so rashly. He was a fool, but not for the reason that he thought. Despite the best efforts of his grandmother, his knowledge of the old language wasn't what it should have been. The spell he had found in that old book of hers was not supposed to reverse the curse, but instead transfer it to whoever was responsible for it existing in the first place.

Adrian watched, horrified, as Angela began to scream in front of him. Smoke started to rise up from her body, and the smell of burning flesh overtook the apartment. Her long hair burst into flames, followed by her arms and legs. Within seconds the flames consumed her entire body. It happened so fast there was nothing he could do to stop it. Almost as soon as it had started, the flame died out, and Angela's charred remains fell to the ground with a sickening thud.

It took Adrian a long time to comprehend what had just happened. When he figured it out, he realized that his life from that moment was forever changed. Faced with the possibility of living in perpetual solitude, like poor Angela had been forced to do, he decided instead to walk over to her bathroom. Once there he stared into her mirror and took a second to prepare himself. When he was ready, he spoke aloud to his reflection.

"I love you, Adrian" were the last words he said.

The Catch of the Day

Captain Ishiro roared with disapproval at his men.

"How can you call yourselves fishermen," he screamed, "if you refuse to catch any fish?"

"It is not our fault," protested Sachio, one of his crewmen. "The fish left these waters when the great lizard arose last week to fight the gigantic moth."

Captain Ishiro opened his mouth to speak, but when no argument appeared in his brain he instead slumped down on an empty crate and started to sob into his hands.

"You're right," he wept. "Those monsters have scared away the fish and there is nothing we can do about it but starve!"

This was not the kind of morale-boosting optimism that the crew preferred to hear from the captain. They all looked away from him and went back to work, even though they knew it to be pointless. Together they lowered the large net into the water while Ishiro continued to bemoan his horrible fate.

"I would sell my boat, but who would buy it?" he said to himself. "Who wants a fishing trawler when the ocean has no fish? Why couldn't I have gone into politics like my father wanted? He told me that I would regret the life of the sea and he was right!"

The other crewmen all looked over at Sachio, who was usually the only person who could cheer the captain up whenever he got like this. Sachio tried to ignore their glances until finally he sighed and spoke up.

"Don't worry, Captain," he said, "the fish will come back. They always do. Remember when the giant lizard arose to fight the giant American ape? We thought the fish would never come back after they fought and fought."

"Without a winner, even," added Miki, another crewman.

"That's right," continued Sachio. "But the fish did eventually come back. We just have to be patient, like we were back then."

"I know," said the captain, "but just once I would like us to not have to be patient. I would like it if our fortune for once was good rather than bad!"

Even Sachio had nothing to say to that. He knew that the captain was right. Over the years the small trawler and its crew had never seemed to catch even the smallest of breaks. They had to work ceaselessly for the little that they had.

The crew grew quiet and the captain got up to sulk by himself at the ship's wheel. Were it not for the lapping of the waves and the seagulls chirping in the sky, the silence would have been impossible to take. Finally it was time to bring up the net, which they did joylessly, knowing there would be virtually nothing in it that they could sell. Still, as they raised it, they had to admit that it was heavier than it had been the last couple of days.

"Maybe we actually got something," suggested Takeo.

"It's probably garbage," muttered the pessimistic Miki.

Sachio looked over the edge of the boat to see what it was and gasped.

"What is it?" asked Takeo.

Sachio rubbed his eyes and shook his head before he looked down one more time to make sure his eyes had not deceived him. They had not.

"Get the captain!" he ordered Miki.

"Why?"

"Just get him!" Sachio shouted impatiently.

"What is it, Sachio?" asked Takeo. "Is it dangerous?"

"I would tell you, Takeo," Sachio explained, "but you will not believe me until you see it for yourself."

"What is going on?" asked the captain.

"See for yourself," said Sachio as the net rose above the side of the ship and its contents became visible to everyone.

Repeating Sachio's first reaction, they all gasped and rubbed their eyes and shook their heads to make sure that their eyes were not deceiving them.

"Is that what I think it is?" stuttered Miki.

"Can it be?" asked Takeo.

"We're going to be rich!" shouted the captain.

There struggling angrily in the confines of the net was a creature that was a hybrid of two very different species. Its top half looked exactly like a beautiful woman with green hair and skin, and its bottom half was a fishy tail that was at that moment swishing ferociously in the air.

"It's a mermaid!" Miki shouted, stating the obvious.

"Be careful!" urged Sachio as they lowered the creature onto the ship's deck. Though she was out of her element, she did not appear to be suffocating.

"She must be able to breathe our air," suggested Takeo.

"Good!" said the captain. "That means she will be alive when we take her to the mainland! That will make her much more valuable."

"Are we going to sell her?" asked Takeo.

"Of course!" answered the captain.

"But why would anyone be interested in a mermaid these days?" asked Miki. "Almost every month the waters bring forth another strange creature."

The captain laughed.

"People will not pay to see her, but they will pay dearly to eat her!"

His crewmen gasped at this.

"Eat her?" asked a stunned Sachio.

"You don't think this is the first time a mermaid has been caught in these waters, do you?" asked the captain. "There are some men out there who have been lucky enough to feast on a creature such as this, and they will pay almost anything to enjoy its exotic flavor once again. Don't you see? We will earn enough from selling her on the black market that none of us will ever have to fish these treacherous monster-filled waters again!"

"But that's horrible!" protested Takeo. "Who could eat a mermaid?"

"Don't be blinded by what you see!" ordered the captain. "Yes, part of her looks like a beautiful woman, but that is simply a trick of nature and nothing more. Like the blowfish that scares off predators by inflating itself to three times its size, this animal's beauty is merely a way to keep us from killing her. It doesn't mean she's part human. She merely looks that way. She is as alien to us as a tuna fish or a mako shark!"

As the captain tried to convince them, the mermaid stopped thrashing about in the net and watched them with sad, terrified eyes.

"But look at her," Sachio countered. "Can't you see the fear in her eyes? That is not the gaze of a mindless animal—there is thought behind it."

"A cow thinks, too," argued the captain. "Does that keep you from eating beef? I once saw a pig on television who could do math as well as a child of seven, but that didn't stop me from eating pork."

"But that is different," said Miki.

"How?"

The crew all tried to answer him, but none of them could think of a good reason.

As they hesitated, the creature in the net began to speak. What came from her mouth sounded like no language they had ever heard, but there was no denying that it sounded like a language.

"There!" Sachio shouted triumphantly when she finished. "Cows and pigs cannot speak! Listen to her! A mindless animal could not sound like that!"

The captain was unconvinced.

"It sounds like nonsense to me."

"So what?" said Takeo. "I cannot understand Spanish or French or English. That does not mean it's okay for me to eat people who speak those languages."

"I am not asking you to eat the creature!" argued the captain. "We will merely sell her to the black market. What happens to her then is none of our concern."

"But—" Sachio started.

"Enough!" the captain interrupted angrily. "I am the captain of this boat and I am the one who makes the decisions! If you don't like it you can quit now and forfeit your share of the money!"

The three men all looked at each other and then at the lovely creature in the net. Ashamed, they bowed their heads and said nothing.

"It is settled, then," said the captain. "We will sell her as soon as we get to the mainland." He looked up to the sky and saw that the sun was starting to set. "If we leave now we will get there just before dawn."

"What do we do with her until then?" asked Miki.

"Throw her where we throw all the other fish," ordered the captain.

Without any enthusiasm the three men untangled the mermaid and lifted her out of the net. At first she seemed grateful, but when it became clear that they weren't going to free her she started to cry. Her tears wounded them all, but they followed the captain's orders and placed her gently into the deep metal hold where they kept all their catches.

"At least there's some water in there," said Takeo. "That'll make her more comfortable than she was up here on the deck."

"Cover it up," shouted the captain, who had returned to his position at the ship's wheel.

The mermaid began to plead and beg in her strange language as they covered the hold with a heavy plastic tarp. All three of them were crying by the time that they were done.

"This isn't right," said Sachio.

"No, it isn't," agreed Takeo, "but sometimes life doesn't allow you to do the right thing."

Miki nodded. "Takeo is right. If we were richer, smarter men then we could save her, but we are poor and we are stupid and if we let her go we will stay that way forever."

"You're right," sighed Sachio as they walked away from the hold and the cries of their captured beauty.

As the sun faded completely away and the night sky took over above them, they sat wordlessly and ate a meager dinner of rice and miso soup. Usually they would stay up after that and tell stories or play games, but no one felt like having any fun so they just went to sleep. Captain Ishiro stayed behind the wheel, determined to bring his exotic catch to shore before the sun rose again.

All three men dreamed the same dream. In it the beautiful creature called to them by singing a heartbreaking song. Though they could not understand the words, they all knew what the song meant. It told the true story of a mermaid who fell in love with a handsome fisherman, only to have him sell her to an evil emperor who served her broiled to his court on a silver platter. At the song's end they all awoke at once, knowing that if they did not act, then the story in the song would happen once again.

They jumped out of their cots and ran to the hold, only to find their captain waiting for them with a gun in his hand.

"You think I did not hear her song?" he asked them. "Do not be fooled. She does not love you; she merely wants you to set her free. I won't let that happen."

"There's three of us," threatened Sachio. "You can't shoot us all."

"I'll shoot who I have to!" the captain shouted.

The three men looked at each other and with a nod of Sachio's head they rushed toward the captain, who fired blindly at them with his weapon.

Takeo and Miki screamed as stray bullets hit them. They both fell, and their blood began to cover the ship's deck.

Sachio made it to the captain and slapped the gun out of his hands. He then threw the captain to the side and started to remove the tarp from on top of the hold.

"Stop it!" demanded the captain who climbed uneasily back to his feet and ran to Sachio, who moved away at the last second, causing Ishiro to fall over the edge of the hold.

The captain splashed into the water and came face-to-face with his prisoner. She looked at him and smiled the most captivating smile he had ever seen. If he had been a young boy and he had seen that smile on a young woman as she passed by him on the street, then he would have remembered it every day for the rest of his life. As it was, he remembered it for the 10 seconds that passed before her widening lips revealed a set of teeth as sharp and deadly as a row of razor blades. He screamed as she lunged at him and sunk her fangs into his throat.

Sachio looked down over the edge of the hold and watched as the creature ate through the captain's neck until his head was no longer attached to his body. Holding her prize she looked up at him and smiled the same smile that had so transfixed the captain just a minute before.

Confused beyond comprehension by what had just happened, he turned away from the hole and stumbled toward his fallen crewmates. Both of them were dead. Before he could start to cry, he heard the sound of screeching thunder in the distance. He looked up and saw Tokyo. There the giant lizard crushed the few buildings that had been left standing after its last battle, as it fought against a golden three-headed dragon.

"I don't understand this world," Sachio sighed.

He turned back to the hold and threw down a rope to the creature. It took all of his strength, but he eventually lifted her out. When she was on the deck she smiled at him again and he flinched, afraid that he was about to meet the same painful fate of his captain, but instead she gave him a sweet and gentle kiss before she hopped over the side of the boat and splashed to freedom.

Sachio looked down at the headless body that floated in the hold and then at the lifeless figures of Takeo and Miki. There would be an investigation and he wouldn't be able to explain any of this. He heard laughter and he turned toward it. It was the mermaid. She giggled in the water below him and beckoned him to join her.

"But I'll drown," he tried to explain to her.

She laughed again and shook her head. She would make sure he didn't drown.

He turned and took a final look at the horrible carnage behind him before he laughed and stripped out of his clothes.

The water was warm as he splashed into it and the mermaid took his hand. She laughed and smiled at him and said something that sounded beautiful, even if he had no idea what it meant.

For her part the mermaid was greatly amused. Of all the times she had gone out to catch some food for her family, this had easily been the most interesting.

The End

GHOST HOUSE BOOKS

Add to your ghost house collection with these books full of fascinating mysteries and terrifying tales.

NEW APRIL 2004

Haunted Battlefields *by Dan Asfar*

Battlefields are places where concentrated suffering and death haunt visitors, long after the cannons are silenced and the dead are laid to rest. These stories explore the wartime exploits of heroes, cowards and civilians, as well as the ghosts that act as lasting reminders of battlefield casualties. Included are tales about the Civil War, the Revolutionary War, the War of 1812 and many others.

$10.95USD/$14.95CDN • ISBN 1-894877-43-8 • 5.25" x 8.25" • 216 pages

NEW MAY 2004

Urban Legends *by A.Ş. Mott*

This book collects many of the intriguing modern myths that persistently do the rounds at water coolers all over, from the vanishing hitchhiker to the tarantula crawling out of the bananas at the local grocery store. Great fun—you'll likely recognize a tale or two you've told friends yourself!

$10.95USD/$14.95CDN • ISBN 1-894877-41-1 • 5.25" x 8.25" • 232 pages

NEW JUNE 2004

Victorian Ghost Stories *by Jo-Anne Christensen*

The Victorian era was a golden age of the paranormal. As interest in the unexplained grew, famous writers created fantastic ghost stories and scientists investigated unusual phenomena, reflecting a society on the brink of madness. Join best-selling author Jo-Anne Christensen as she explores the most bizarre and remarkable stories from this fascinating era of haunted history.

$10.95USD/$14.95CDN • ISBN 1-894877-35-7 • 5.25" x 8.25" • 240 pages

NEW AUGUST 2004

Haunted Cemeteries *by Edrick Thay*

Cemeteries are supposed to be places of quiet repose, where the dead are left to their eternal rest. Some spirits, however, just can't sleep. Edrick Thay shares eyewitness accounts set in graveyards around the world, including the vampire-plagued Highgate Cemetery in London and Egypt's ancient Valley of the Kings.

$10.95USD/$14.95CDN • ISBN 1-894877-60-8 • 5.25" x 8.25" • 216 pages